Great Melodies for Solo Ukulele

by Joe Carr

Online Audio   www.melbay.com/22207BCDEB

Audio Track Listing

Track #

1. Tuning
2. Aura Lee
3. Avalon
4. Beautiful Dreamer
5. Camptown Races
6. Swing Low, Sweet Chariot
7. My Darling Clementine
8. Frankie and Johnny
9. Dixie
10. After You've Gone
11. Oh Danny Boy
12. God Rest Ye Merrily Gentlemen
13. Hello My Baby
14. Home on the Range
15. Home Sweet Home

Track #

16. Back Home Again in Indiana
17. Joy to the World
18. My Old Kentucky Home
19. Limehouse Blues
20. Yankee Doodle
21. We Three Kings of Orient Are
22. Just a Closer Walk with Thee
23. The Marine's Hymn
24. The Old Folks at Home
25. Peg of My Heart
26. Scarborough Fair
27. She'll Be Coming 'Round the Mountain
28. Shenendoah
29. Auld Lang Syne

Special thanks to Gerald Jones for his playing on the online audio recording.
Tenor ukulele by Joe Mendel of Mendel Fretted Instruments, Chesterfield, MO.

© 2012 BY MEL BAY PUBLICATIONS, INC.
ALL RIGHTS RESERVED. INTERNATIONAL COPYRIGHT SECURED. MADE AND PRINTED IN U.S.A.
No part of this publication may be reproduced in whole or in part, or stored in a retrieval system, or transmitted in any form
or by any means, electronic, mechanical, photocopy, recording, or otherwise, without written permission of the publisher.

Visit us on the Web at www.melbay.com — E-mail us at email@melbay.com

Contents

Introduction 2	Back Home Again In Indiana 18
Tuning - G C E A 2	Joy To The World 19
Aura Lee 3	*My Old Kentucky Home* 20
Avalon 4	*Limehouse Blues* 21
Beautiful Dreamer 5	*Yankee Doodle* 22
Camptown Races 6	*We Three Kings of Orient Are* 23
Swing Low, Sweet Chariot 7	*Just a Closer Walk With Thee* 24
My Darling Clementine 8	*The Marine's Hymn* 25
Frankie and Johnny 8	*The Old Folks at Home* 26
Dixie 9	*Peg of My Heart* 27
After You've Gone 10-11	*Scarborough Fair* 28
Oh Danny Boy 12-13	*She'll Be Coming 'Round the Mountain* 29
God Rest Ye Merry Gentlemen 14	*Shenendoah* 30
Hello, My Baby 15	*Auld Lang Syne* 31
Home On The Range 16	About the Author 32
Home Sweet Home 17	

Great Melodies for Solo Ukulele

The ukulele is used most often as a rhythm instrument to accompany singing. The infectious rhythm produced by the ukulele provides an attractive background for sing-alongs. The ukulele is also an effective solo instrument carrying both the melody and chords when playing specially arranged music. In the 1920s and 30s, a number of genius string wizards including Roy Smeck and George Formby demonstrated the "uke's" ability to produce a full sound all by itself.

This book includes 28 classic beautiful melodies arranged for solo ukulele. These arrangements sound wonderful played by musicians of all levels. Some arrangements are suited to beginners while others will be best played by more advanced players. Regardless of your previous experience, these arrangements, even played at slow tempos, will produce an attractive full sound.

Each arrangement includes guitar chords that can be played as accompaniment. The given music is correct for soprano, concert and tenor ukuleles tuned in the re-entrant style to G C E A. This music can be played on baritone ukulele also, but the music will sound in a different key and the guitar chords will not be correct. *Re-entrant* refers to the order of notes in the standard "my dog has fleas" ukulele tuning. Instead of ascending low to high, the uke tuning begins with a G note followed by a lower C note. If a player chooses to replace the fourth string with a thicker string and tune it to the G one octave lower than normal, this is referred to as "low G" tuning and the uke tuning then is no longer considered re-entrant. This is a possible but less common way to tune the uke.

These arrangements are designed so that the melody note is either a solo note or the last note of the chord when strummed from the fourth string to the first. Careful tuning is an important part of achieving a good sound. Use audio track 1 to get in good tune before each playing session. If you prefer to use a keyboard, tune the strings to G C E A (Green Cows Eat Apples.) For experienced guitarists, these strings are like the 4th through 1st strings of the guitar capoed at the 5th fret. Alternately, the familiar tune "my dog has fleas" can be used to tune if no standard note source is available. When using this "by ear" method, be careful that the C string is not too loose (bad sound) and the A string is not too tight (it may break).

Aura Lee

This beautiful melody dates from the 19th century and was used as the melody to the Elvis song, *Love Me Tender*.

Avalon

Avalon was a star studded town on Catalina Island off the California coast in the 1920s.

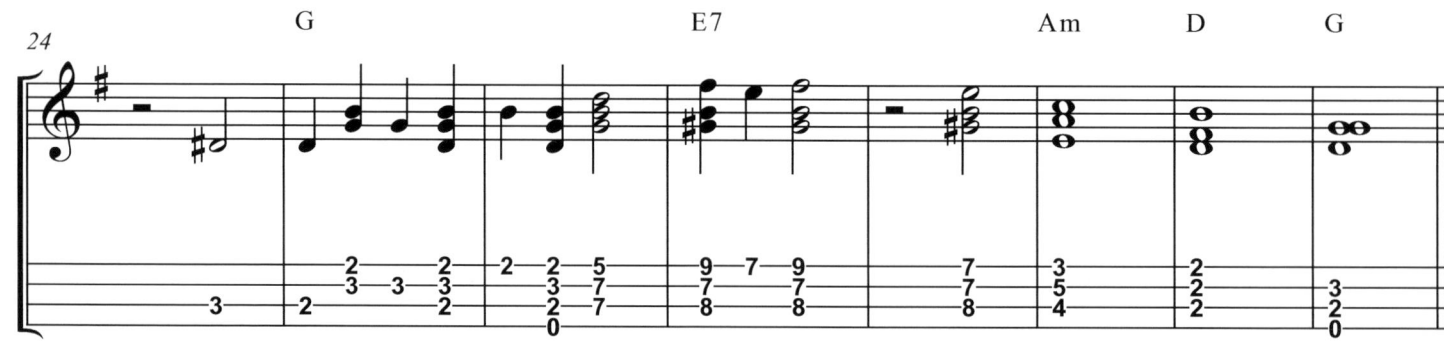

Beautiful Dreamer

Here is one of several beautiful Stephen Foster (1826–1864) songs in this volume. This was the last known song written by him. It was published posthumously in 1864, the year Foster died.

Camptown Races

A Stephen Foster song also called *Camptown Ladies*. It was written in 1850.

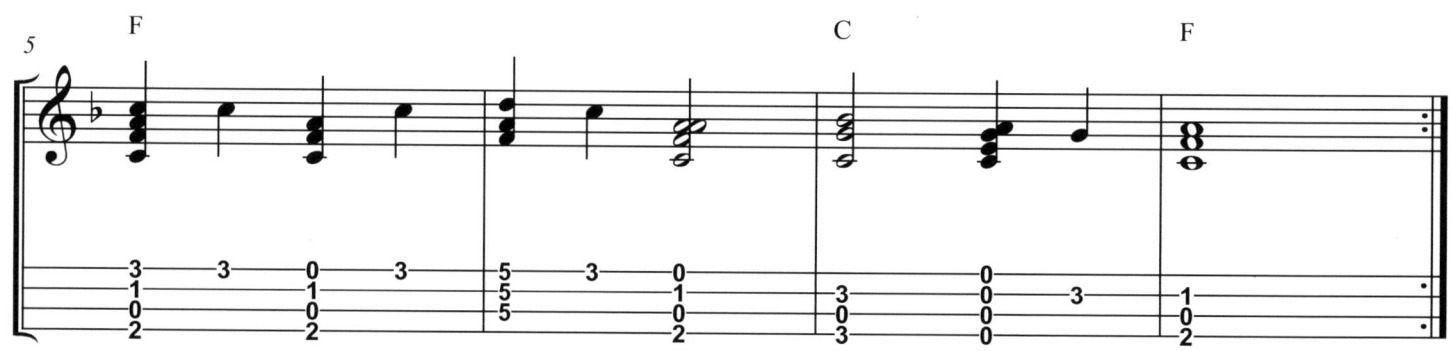

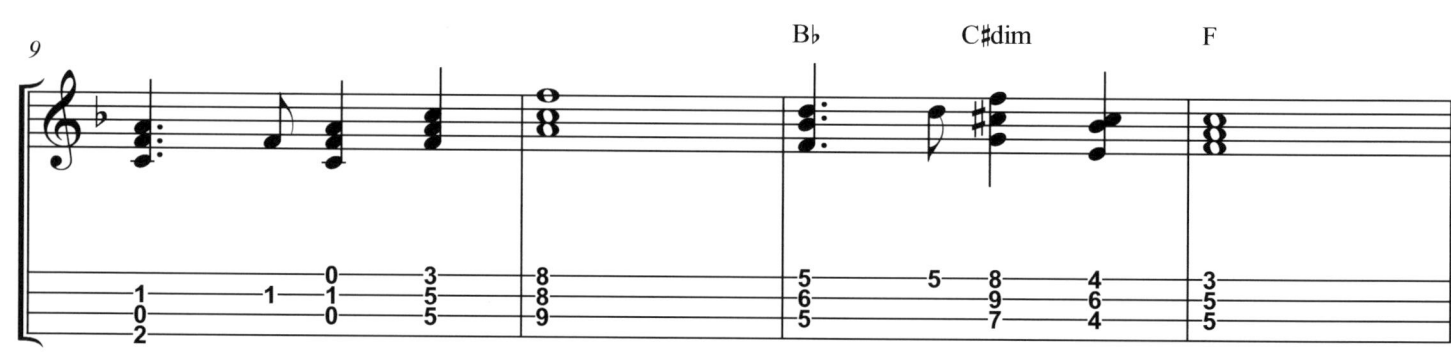

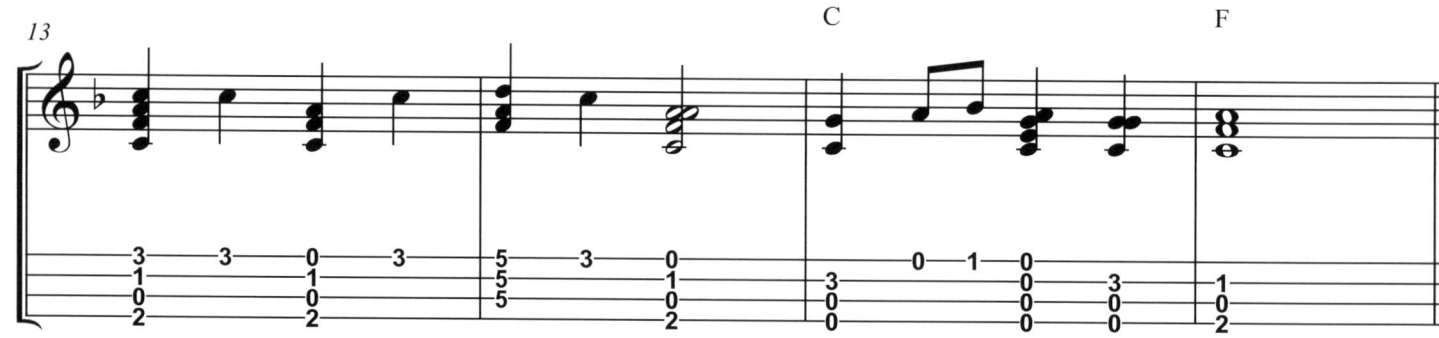

Swing Low, Sweet Chariot

A well known African-American spiritual.

My Darling Clementine

There is some disagreement about the author of this 19th century Western American ballad.

Frankie and Johnny

Published in 1912 in its modern form, the author and whether the song is based on an actual 19th century murder is the subject of much discussion.

Dixie

This classic song about the American South dates at least to the 1850s.

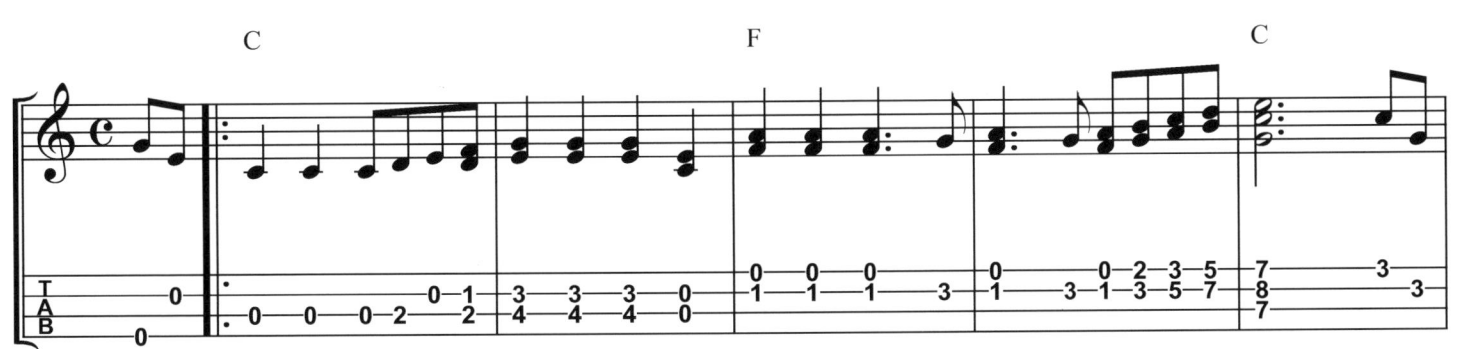
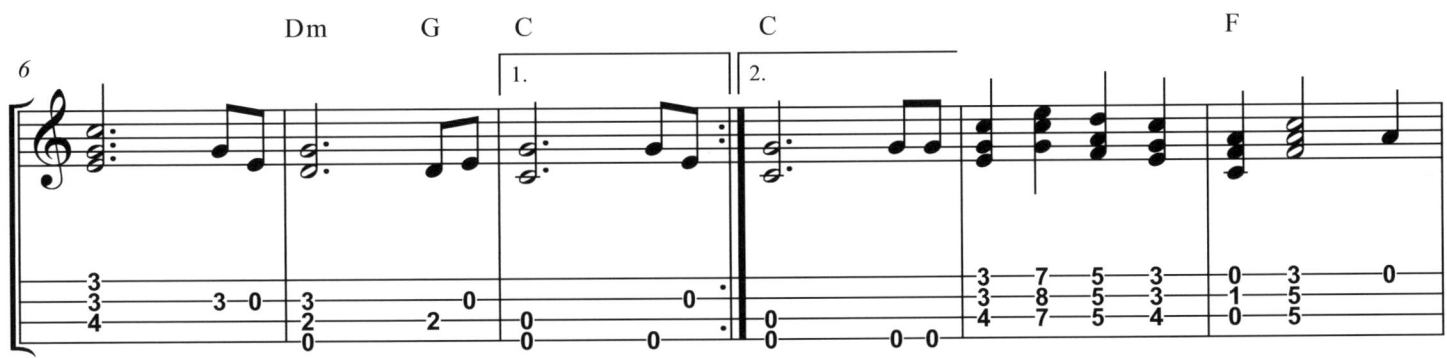
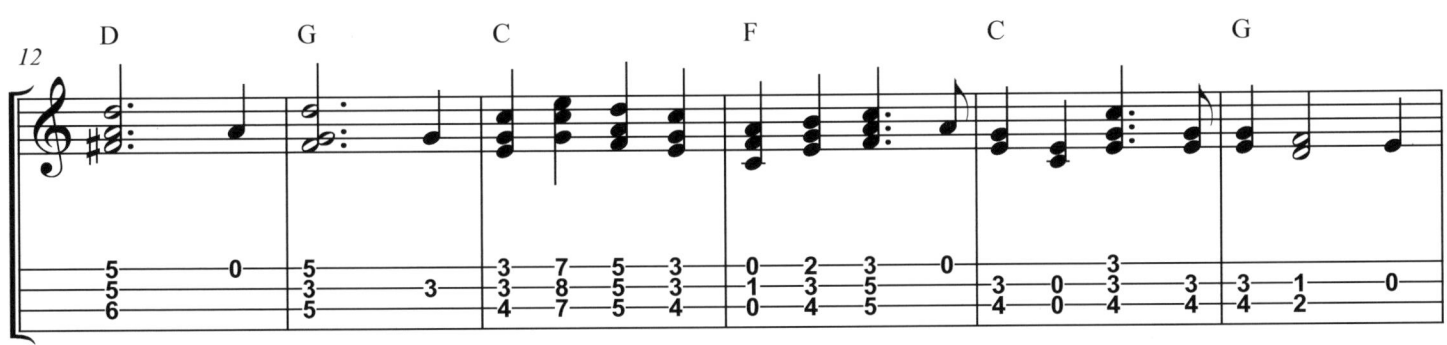
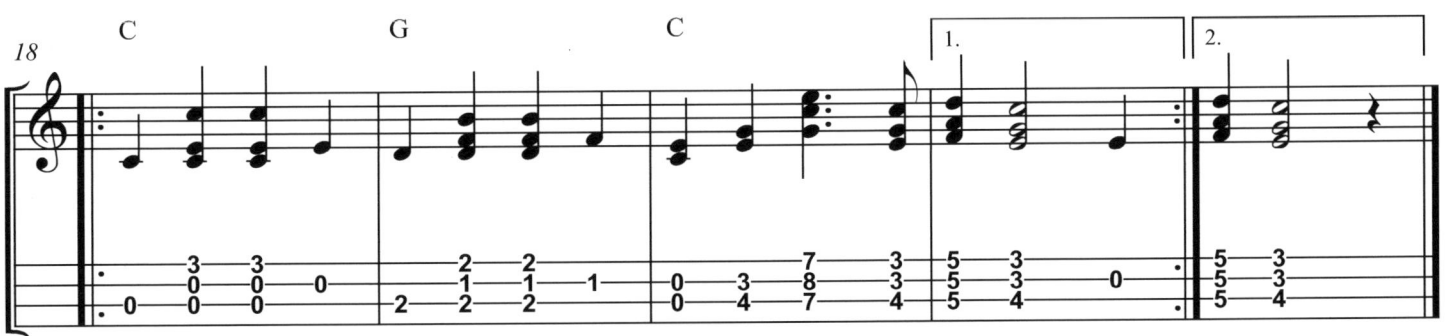

After You've Gone

A 1918 popular song composed by Turner Layton with lyrics written by Henry Creamer.

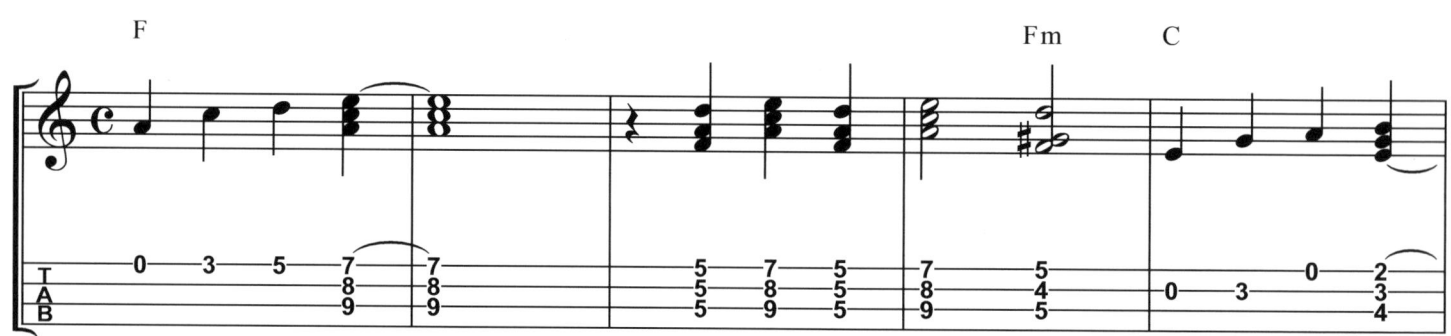

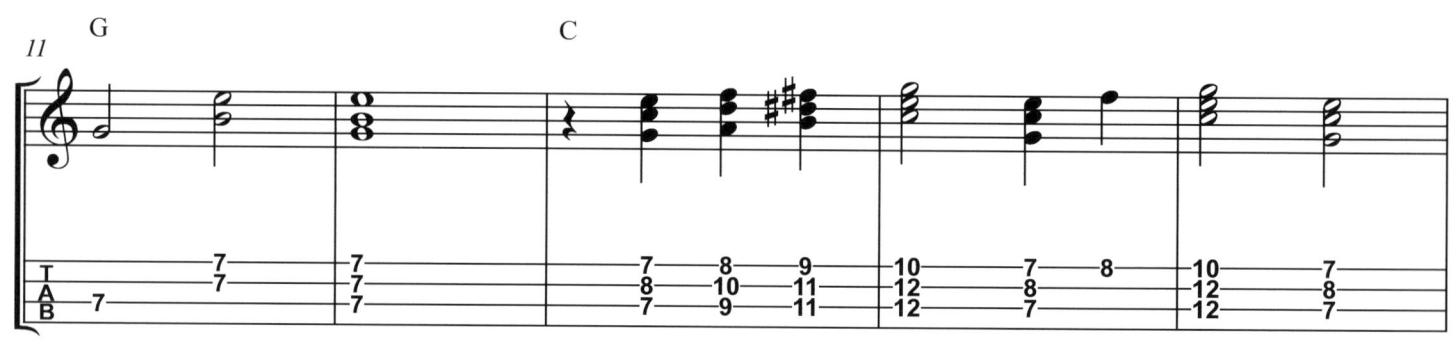

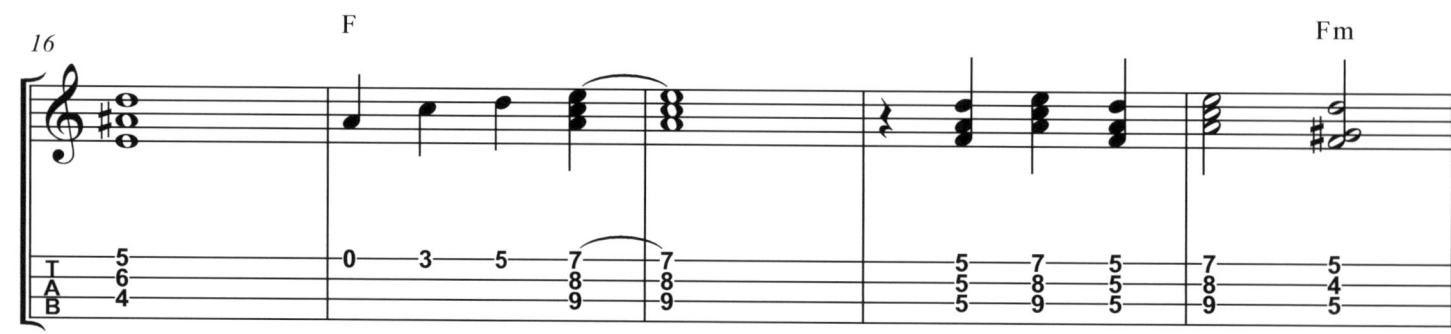

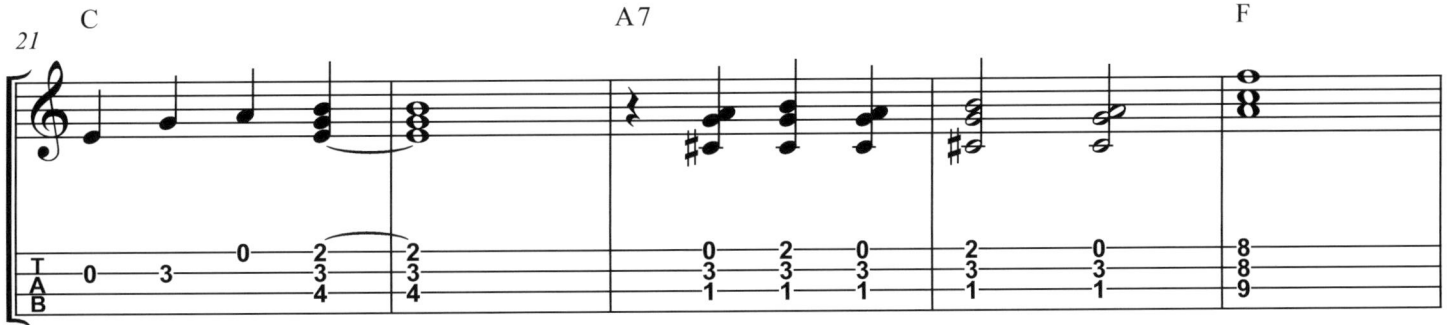
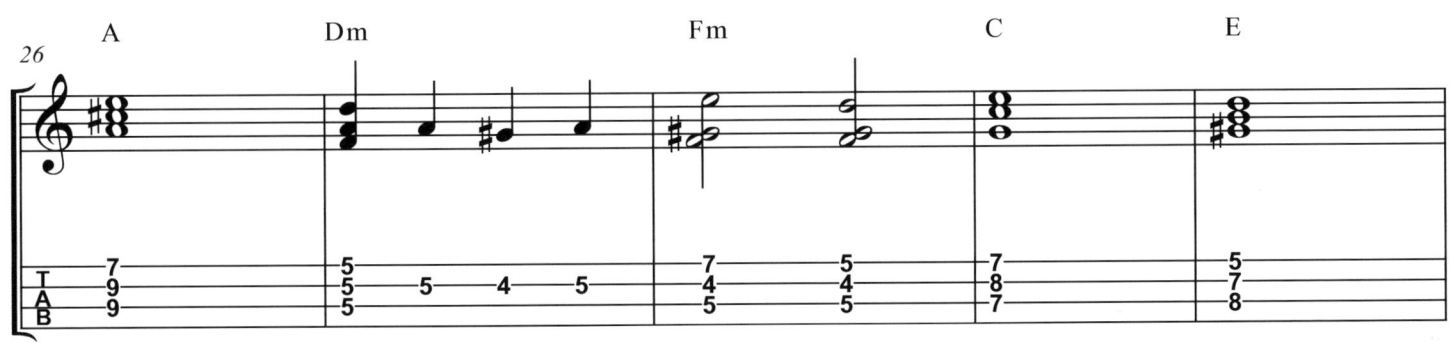
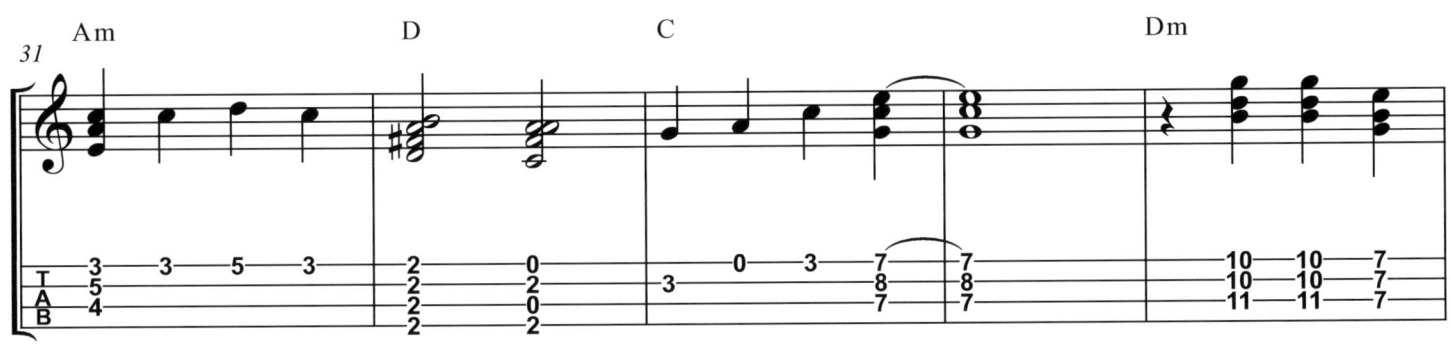
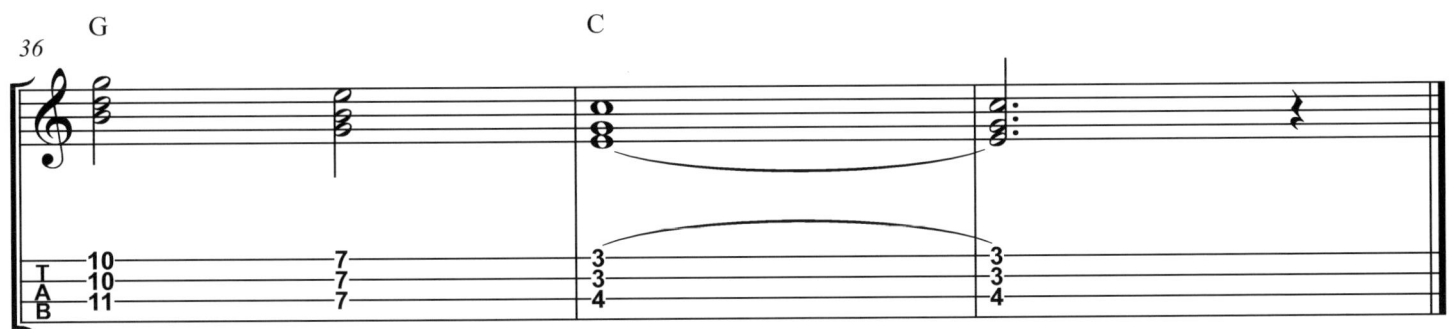

Oh Danny Boy

Also known as "Londonderry Air," a title that has negative political connotations in some circles.

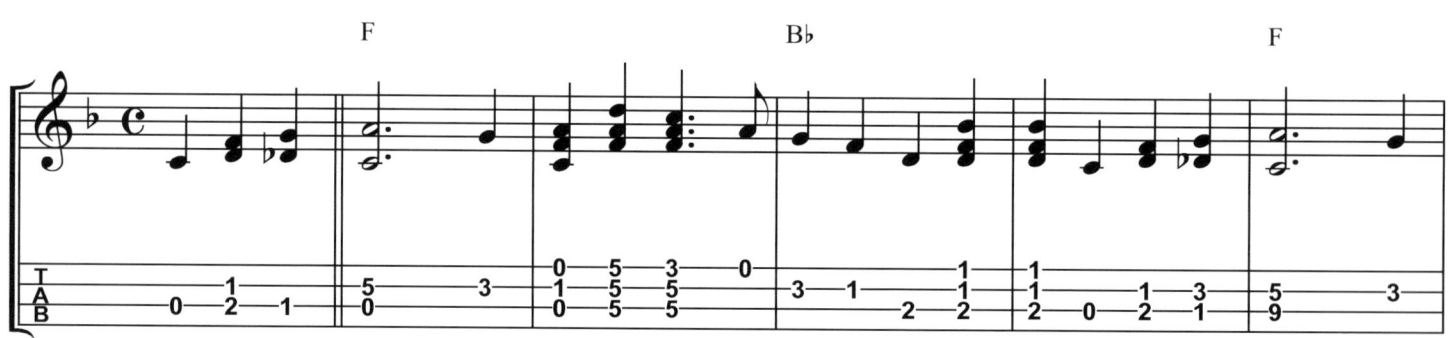
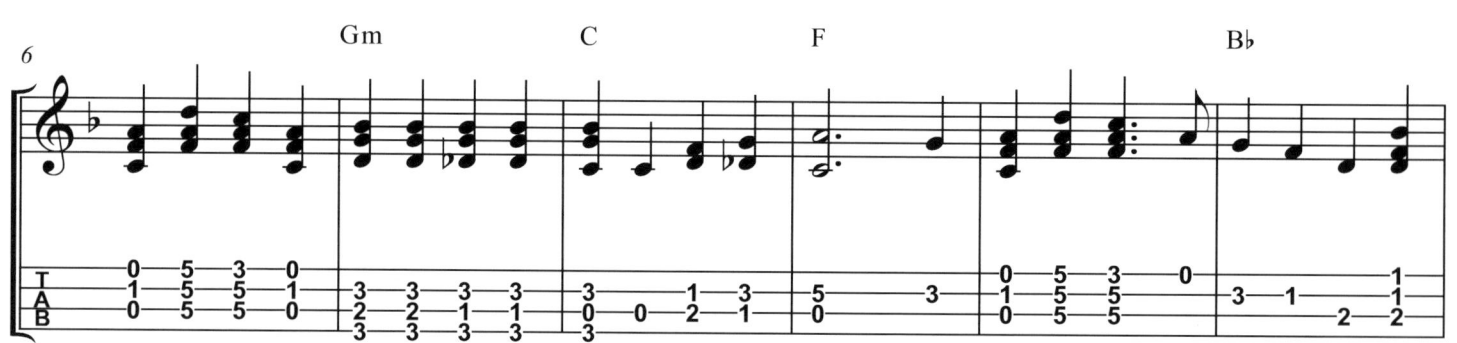
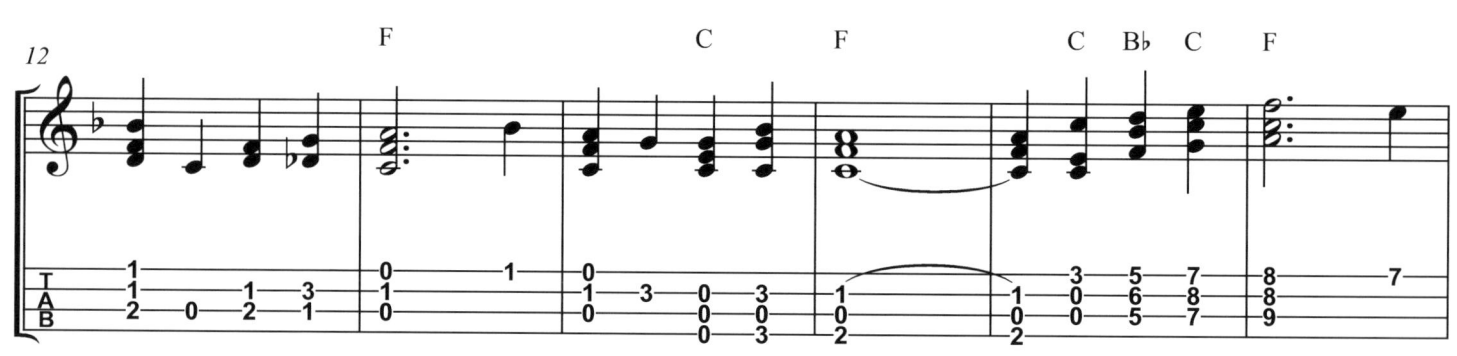
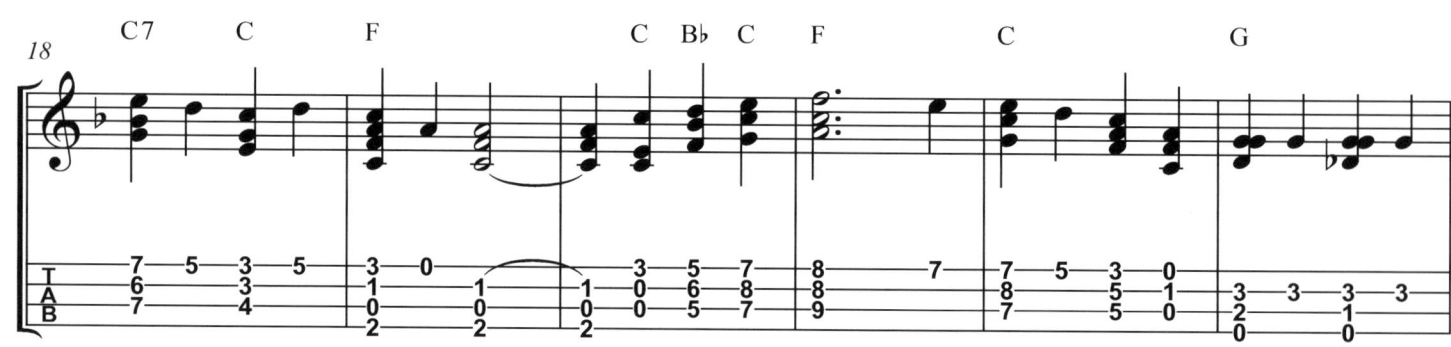

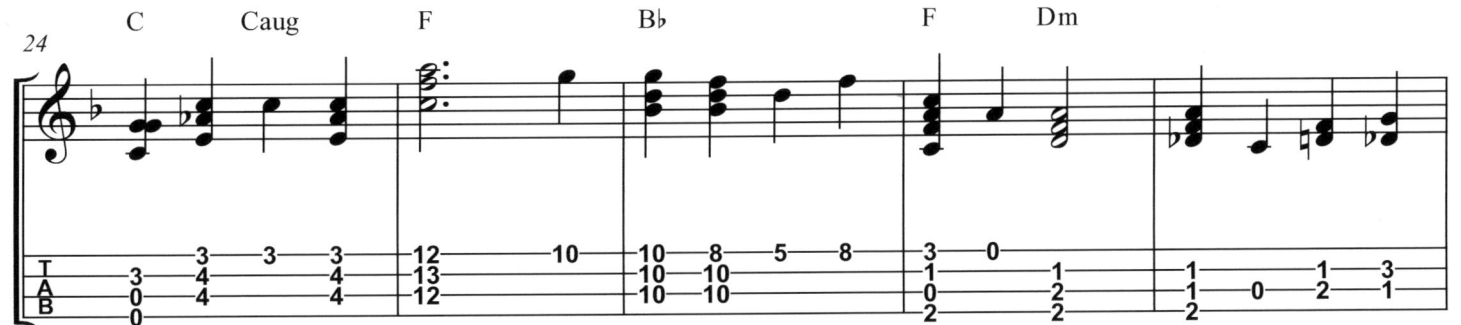
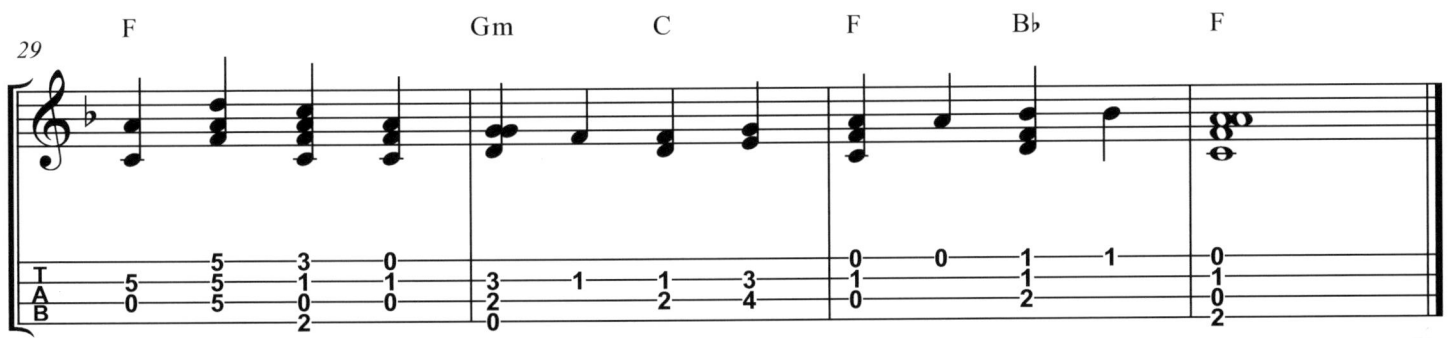

God Rest Ye Merry Gentlemen

Published by William B. Sandys in 1833, this English Christmas carol is referred to by Charles Dickens in his 1843 story *A Christmas Carol*.

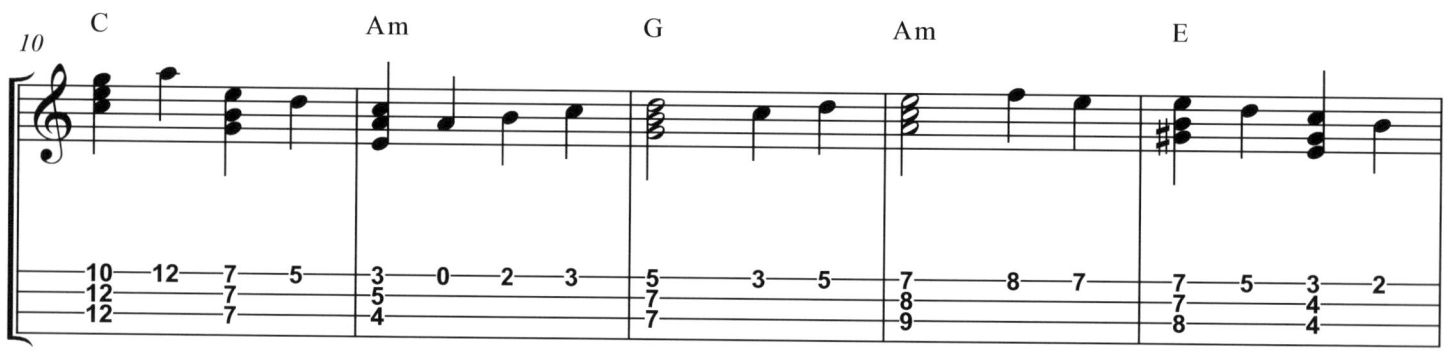

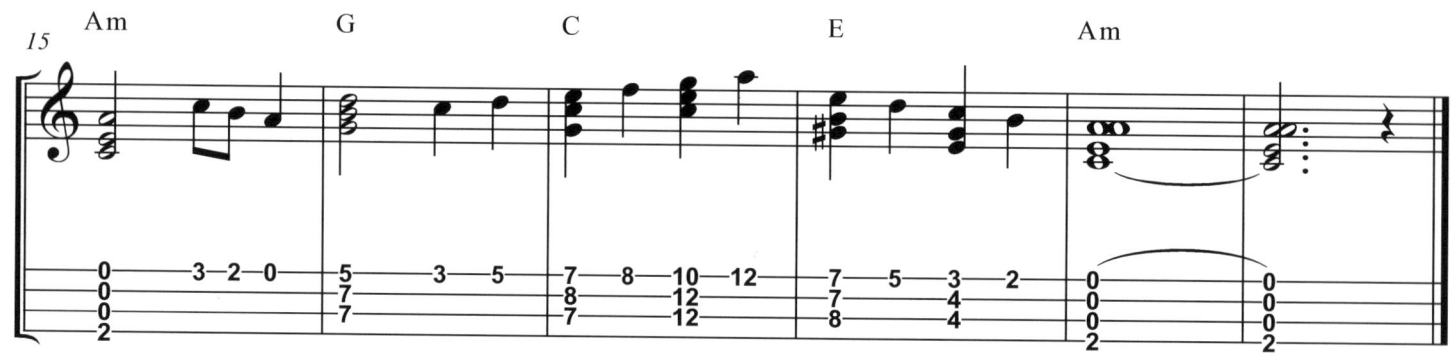

Hello, My Baby

Known to modern audiences primarily for its use in a cartoon, this song was published in 1898 and the lyrics contain a reference to the then new electric device—the telephone.

Home On The Range

The state song of Kansas was written in the 1870s.

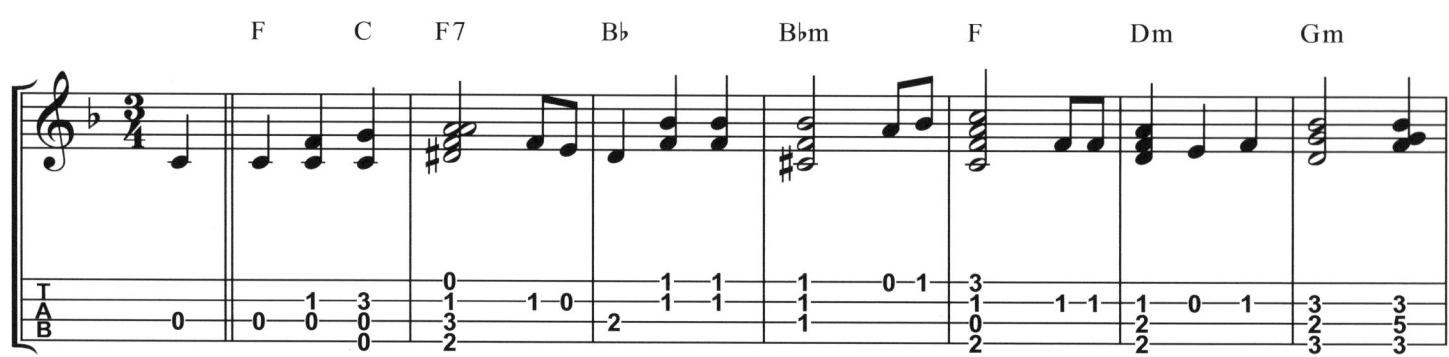

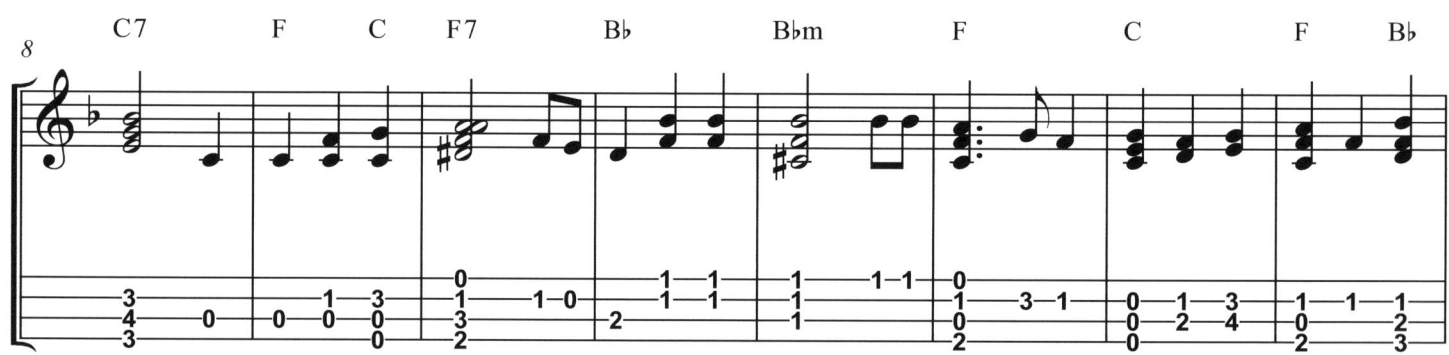

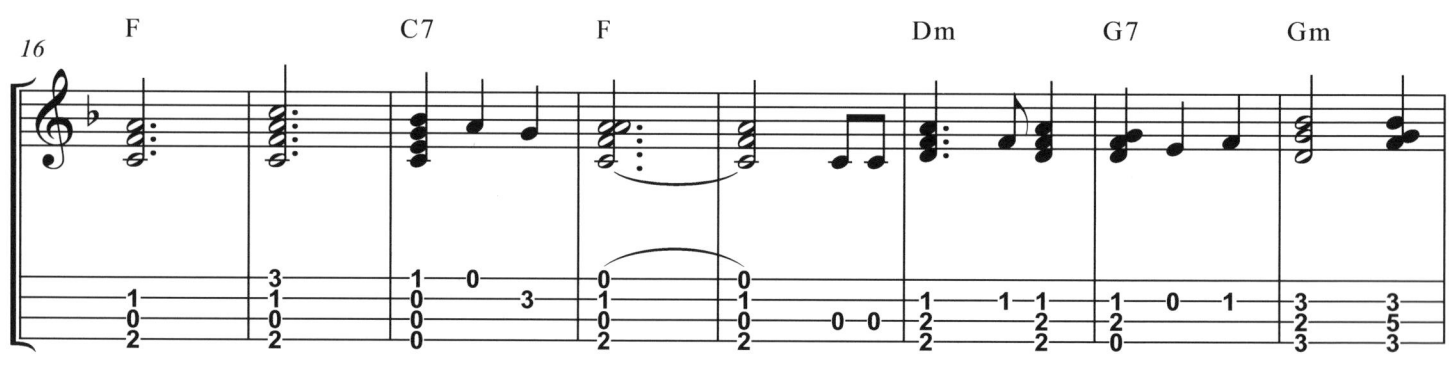

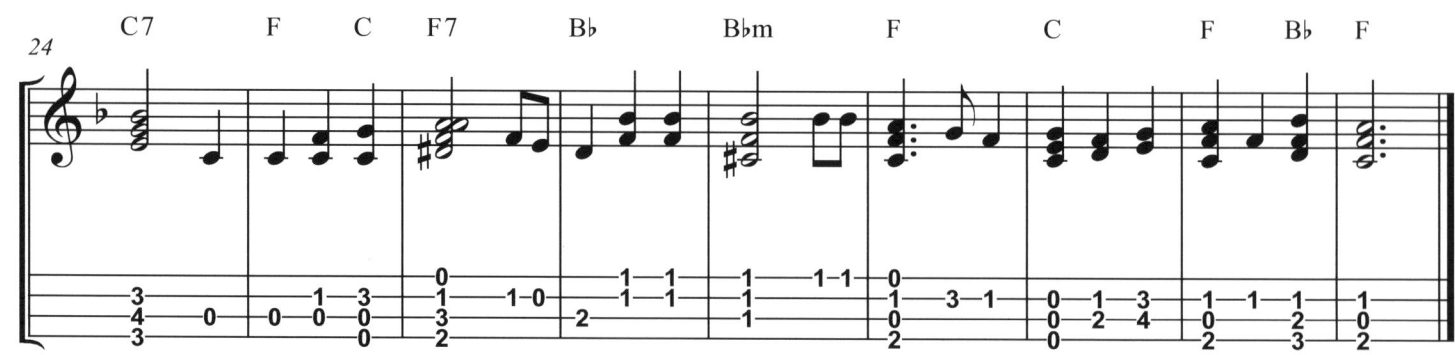

Home Sweet Home

A popular 1852 Stephen Foster song.

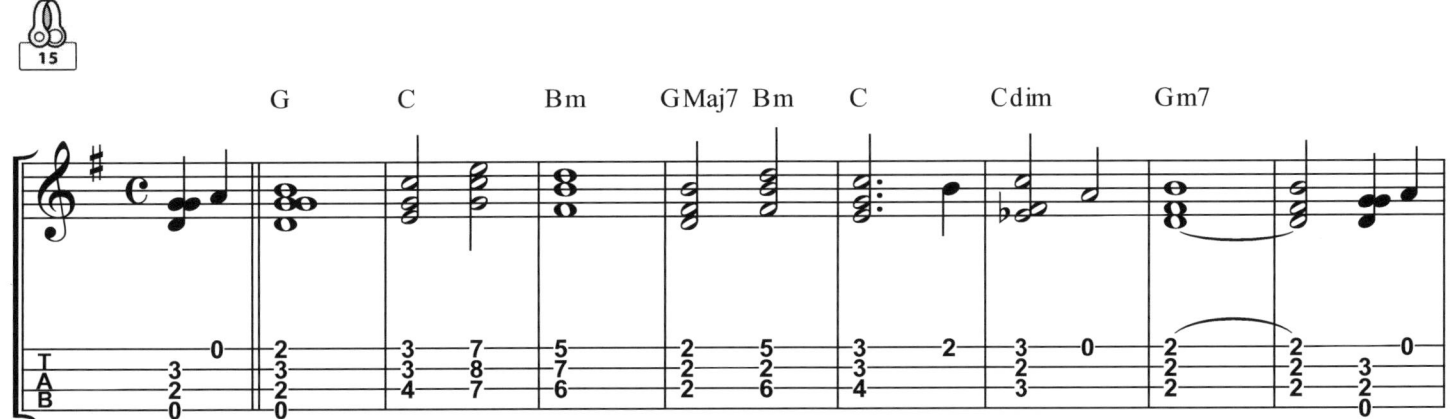
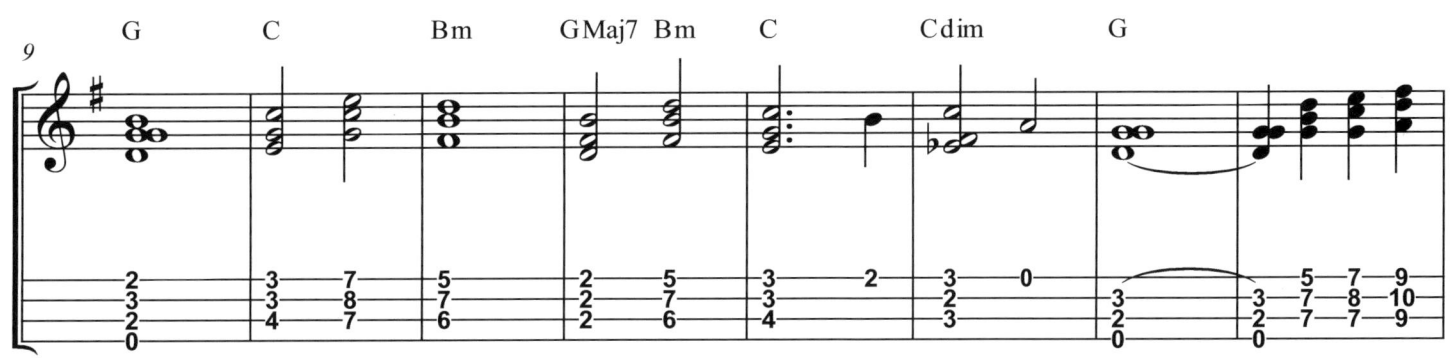
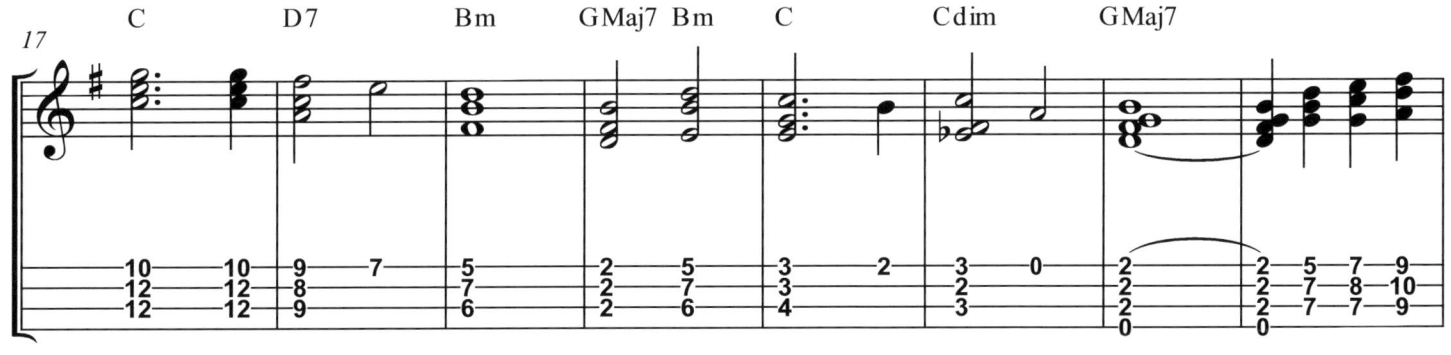
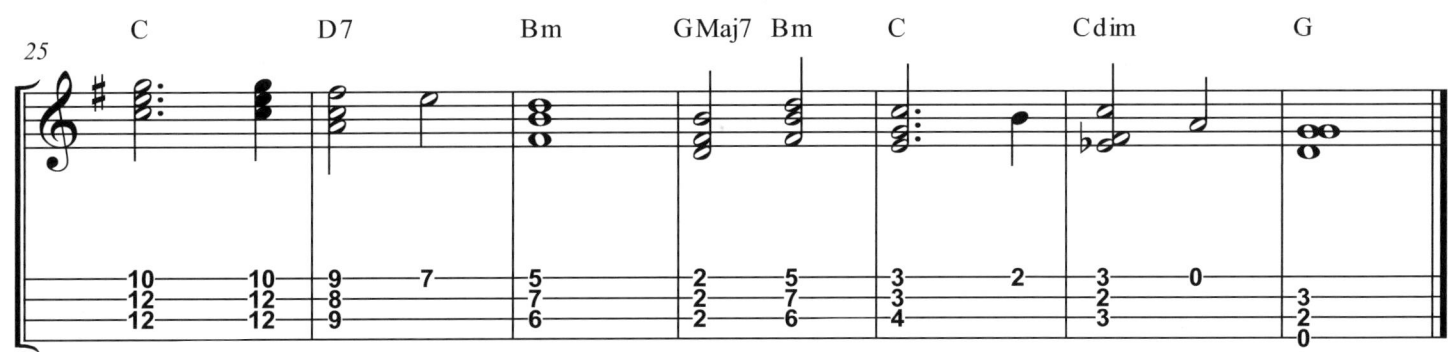

Back Home Again In Indiana

This popular 1917 song is the state song of Indiana.

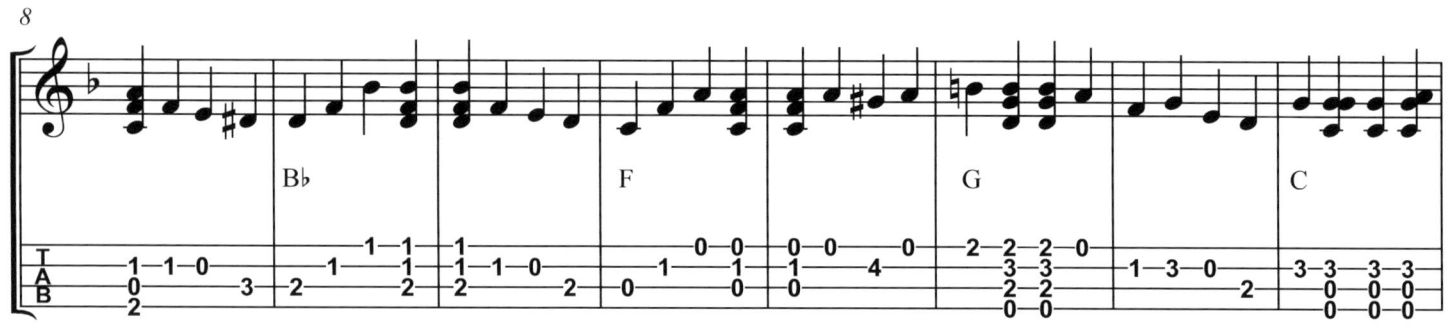
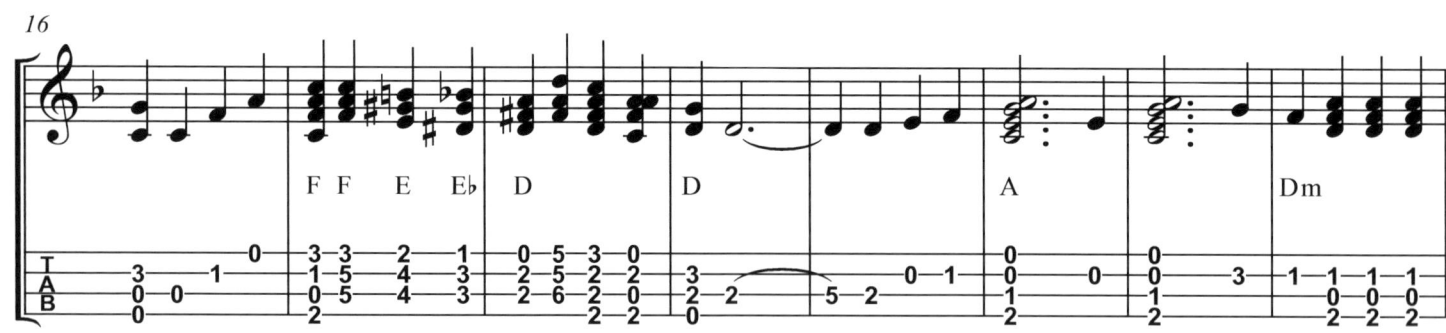
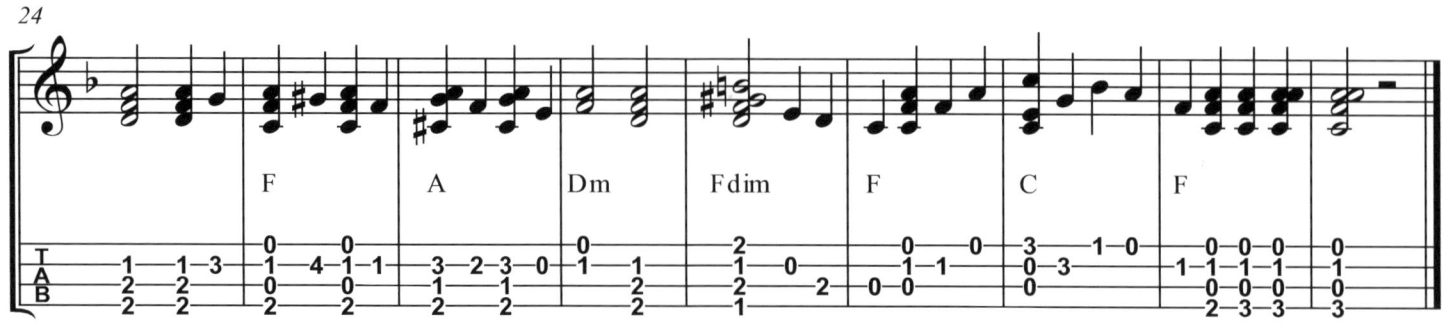

Joy To The World

The music to this well-known Christmas carol was adapted and arranged to English hymn writer Issac Watts' 1719 lyrics by Lowell Mason in 1839.

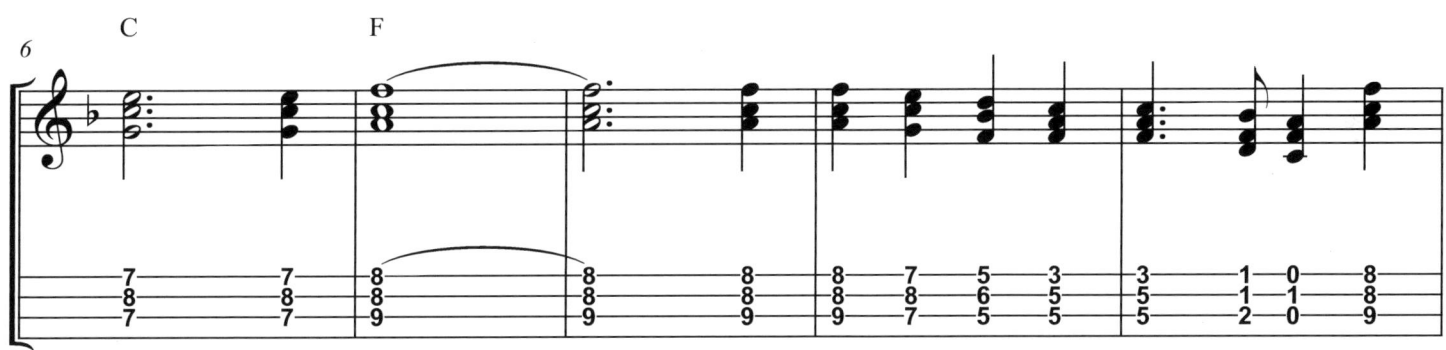
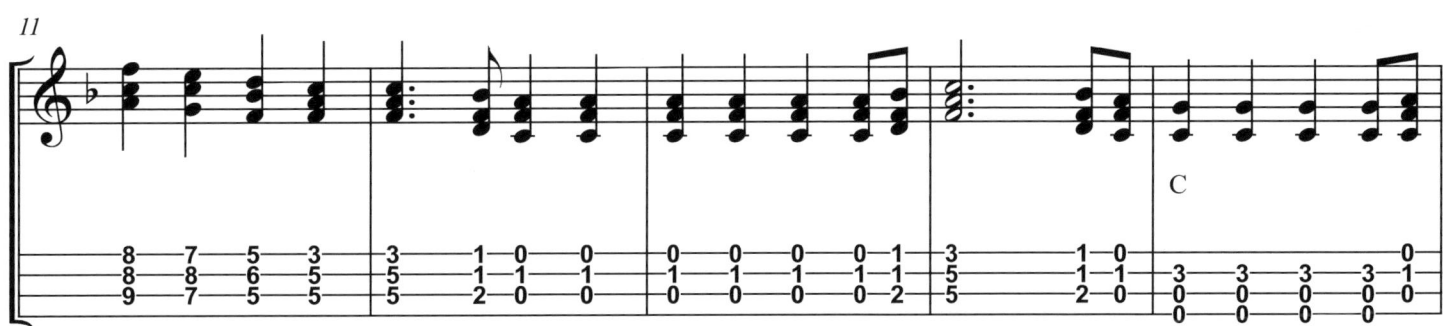

My Old Kentucky Home

Another Stephen Foster favorite, it is the state song of Kentucky. It was published in 1853.

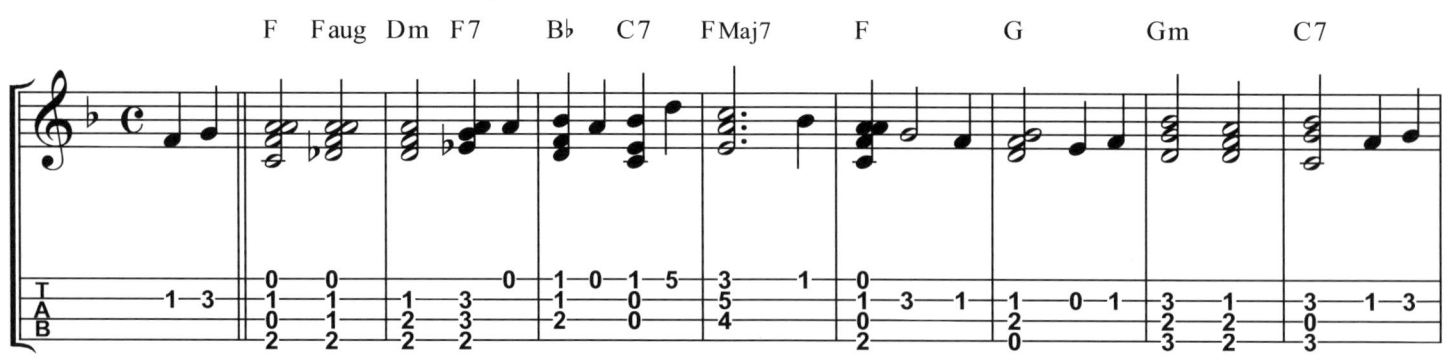

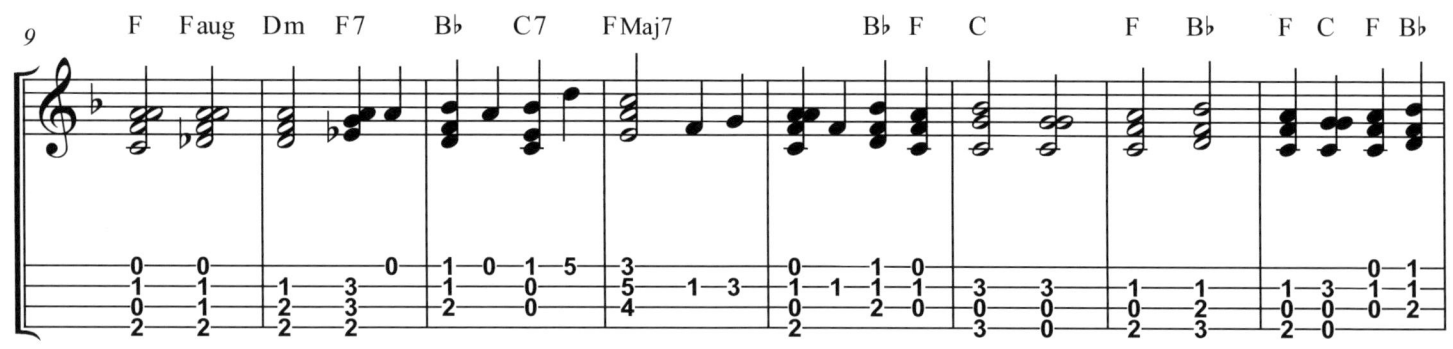

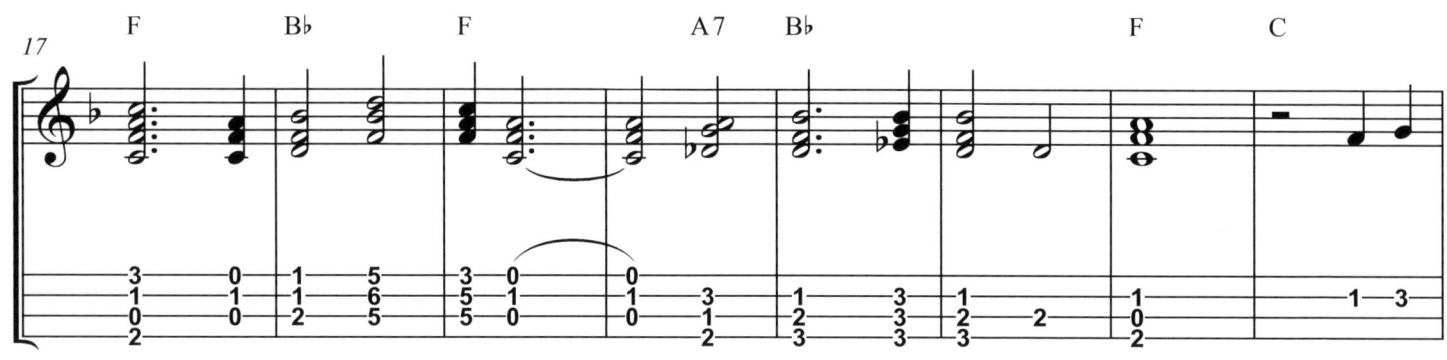

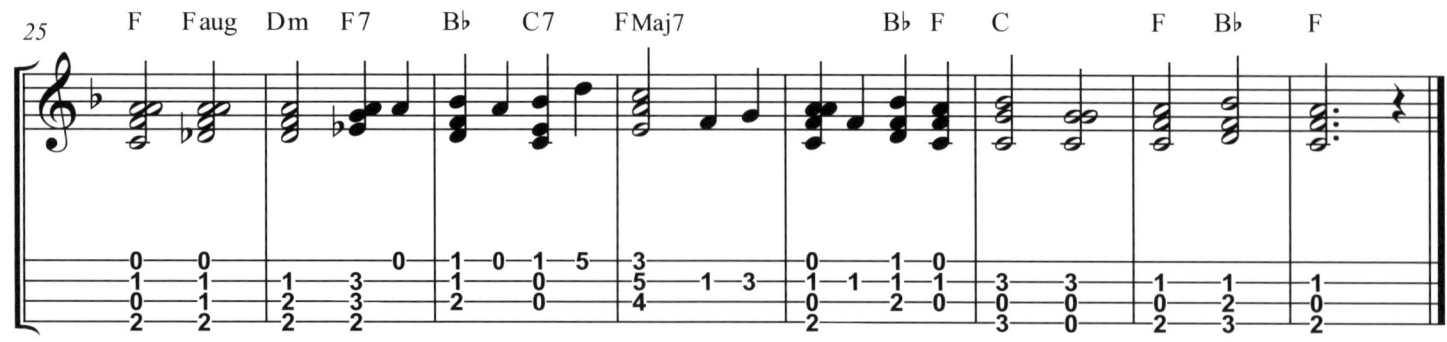

Limehouse Blues

This 1922 jazz standard has been recorded by many.

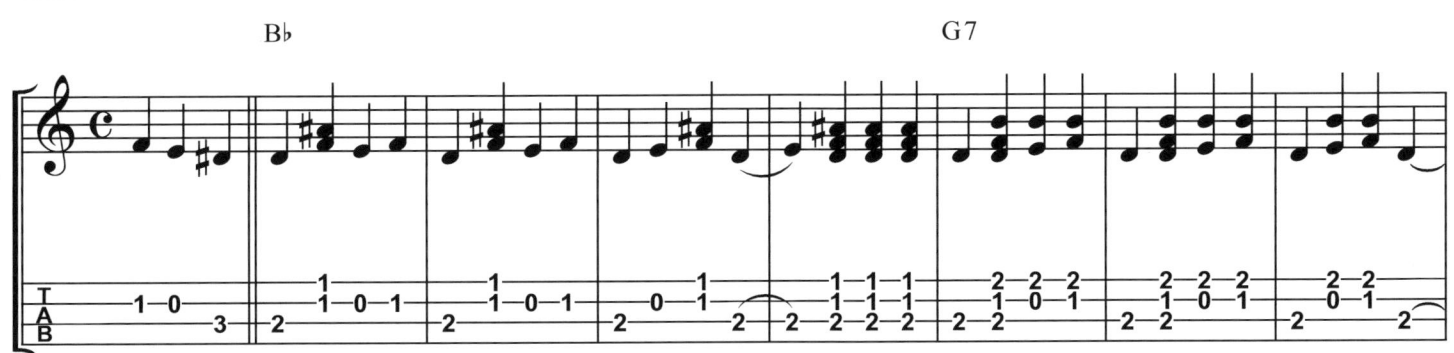

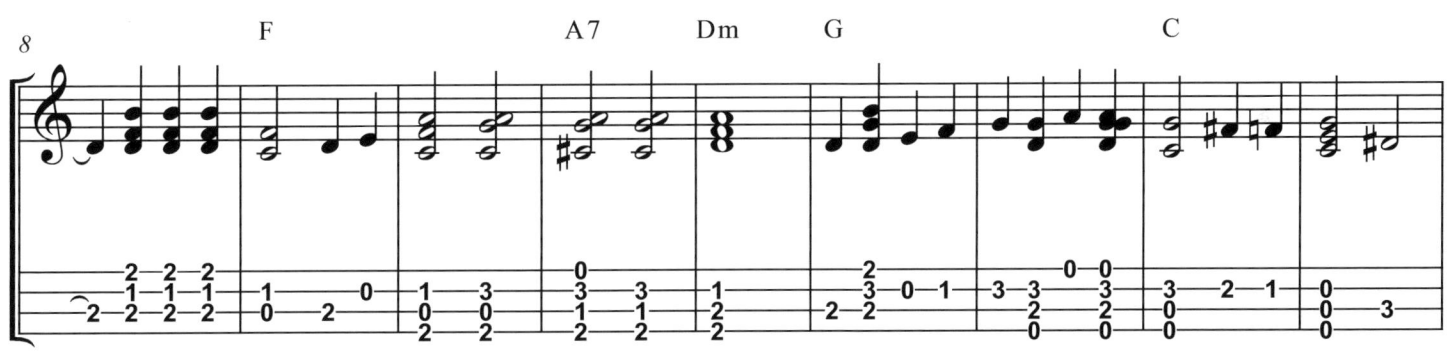

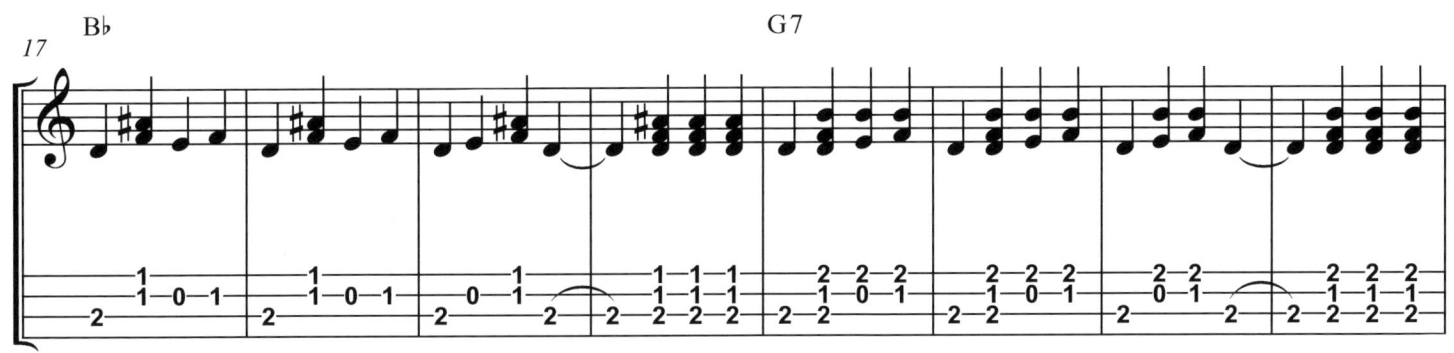

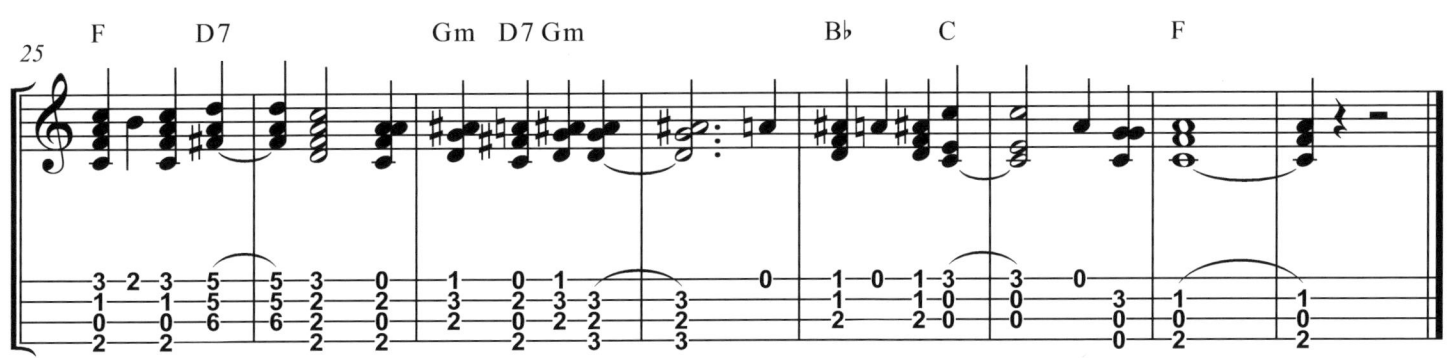

Yankee Doodle

Dating from the mid 1750s, the exact history of this American song is much debated.

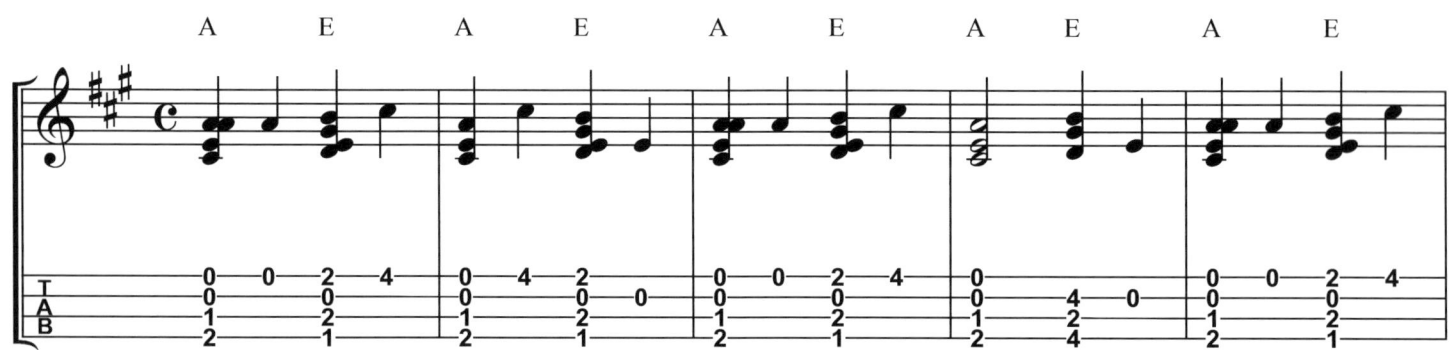

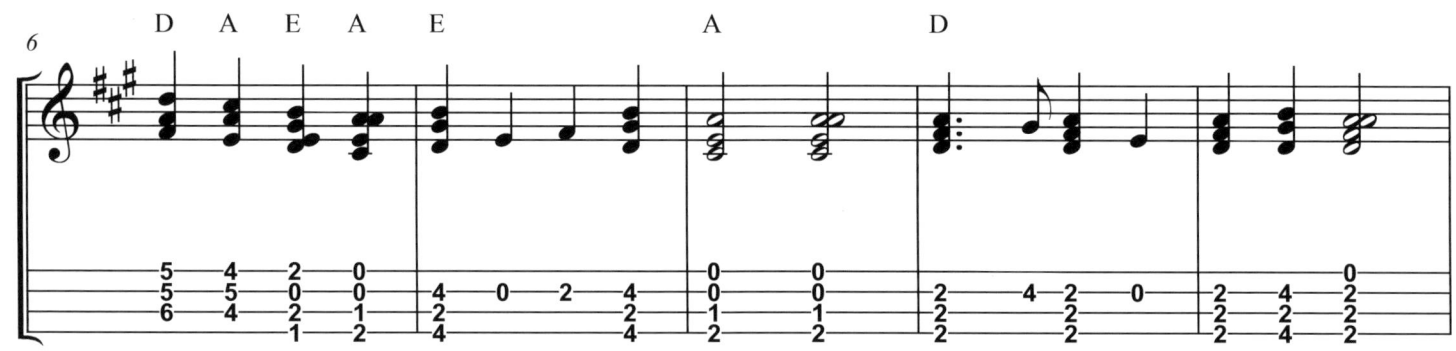

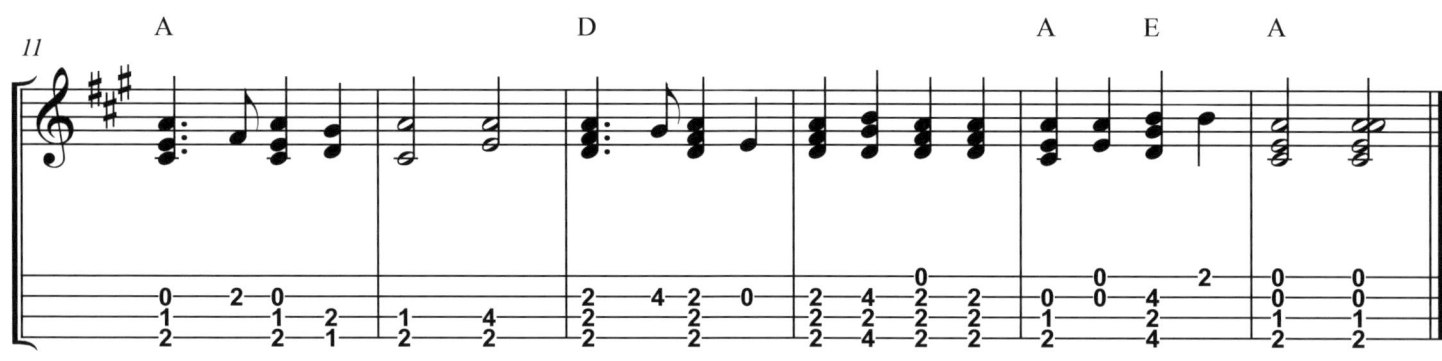

We Three Kings of Orient Are

This Christmas carol was written by the Reverend John Henry Hopkins, Jr. in 1857.

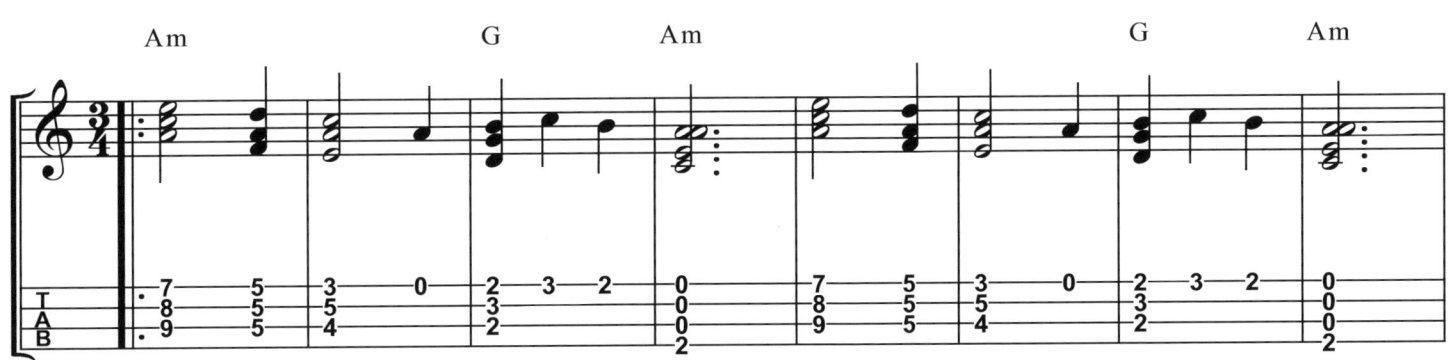

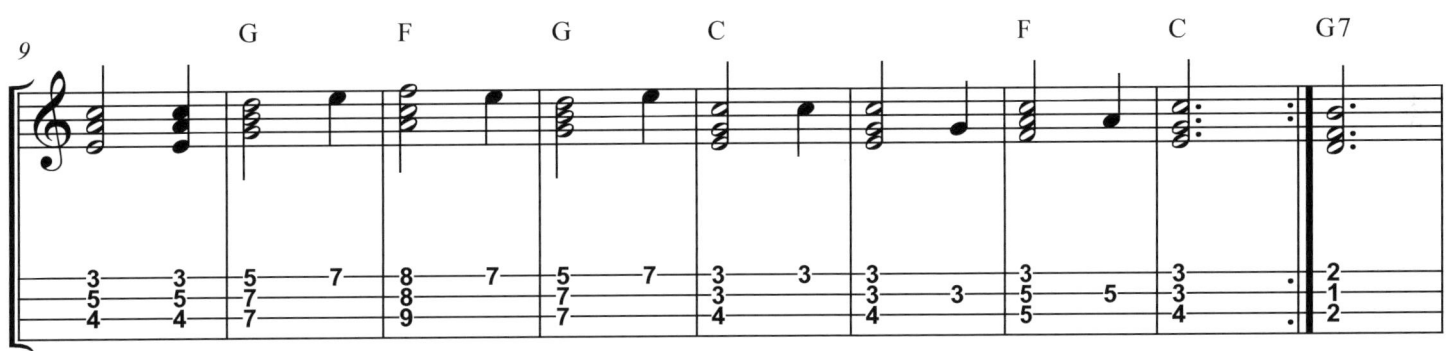

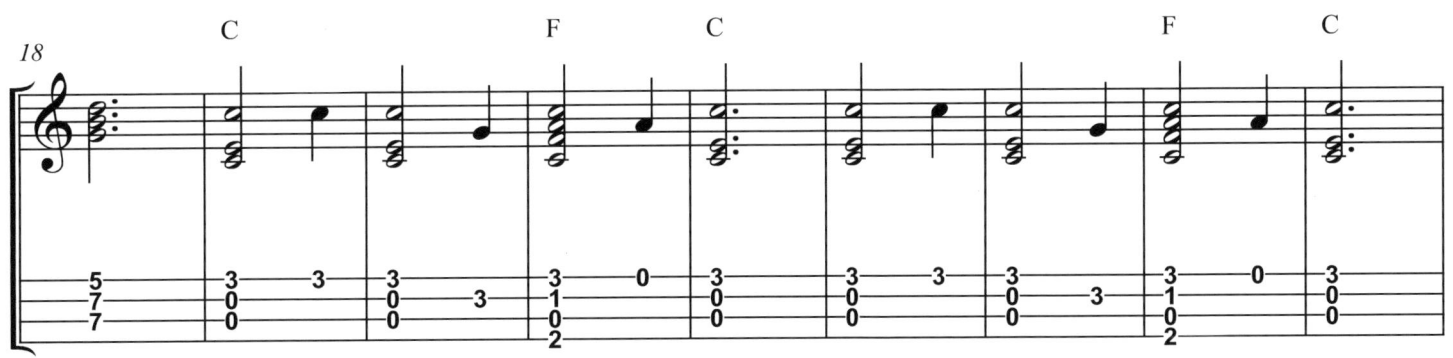

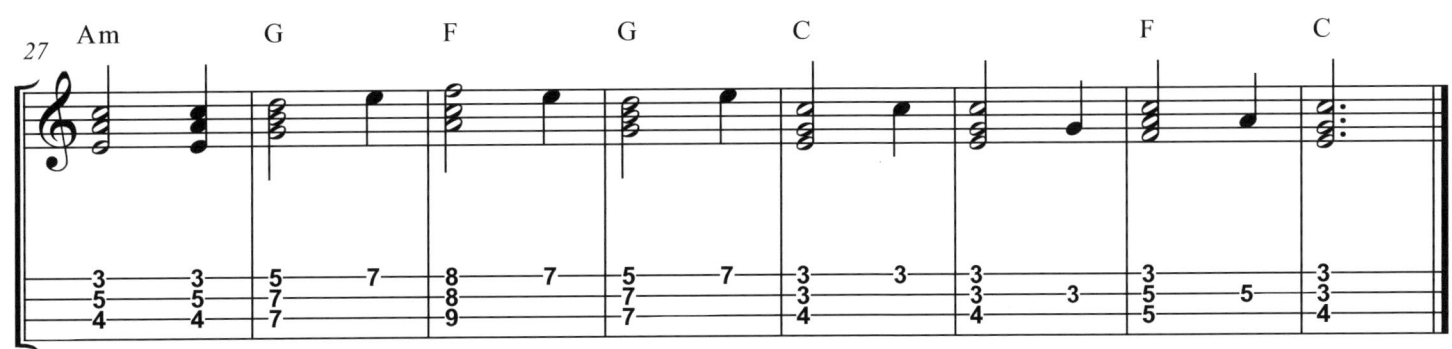

Just a Closer Walk With Thee

The author of this incredibly popular gospel song is unknown.

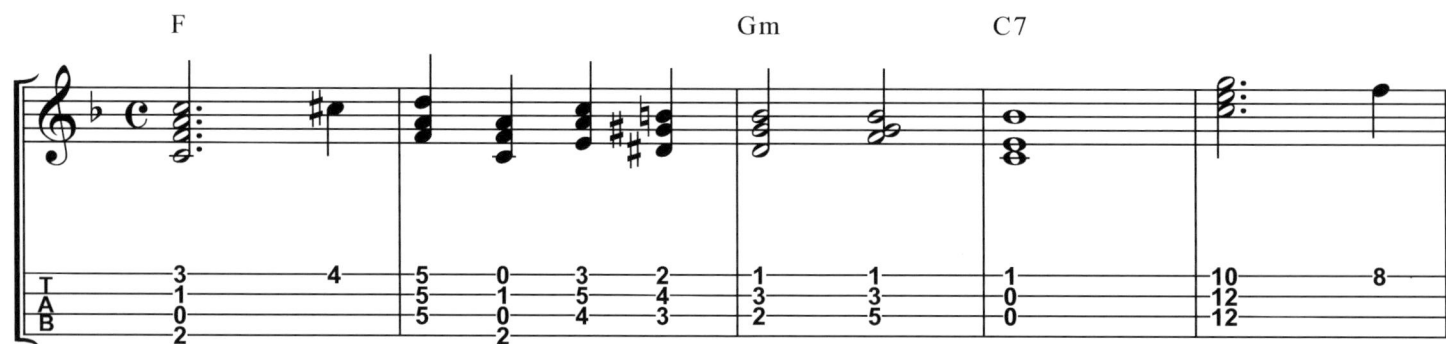

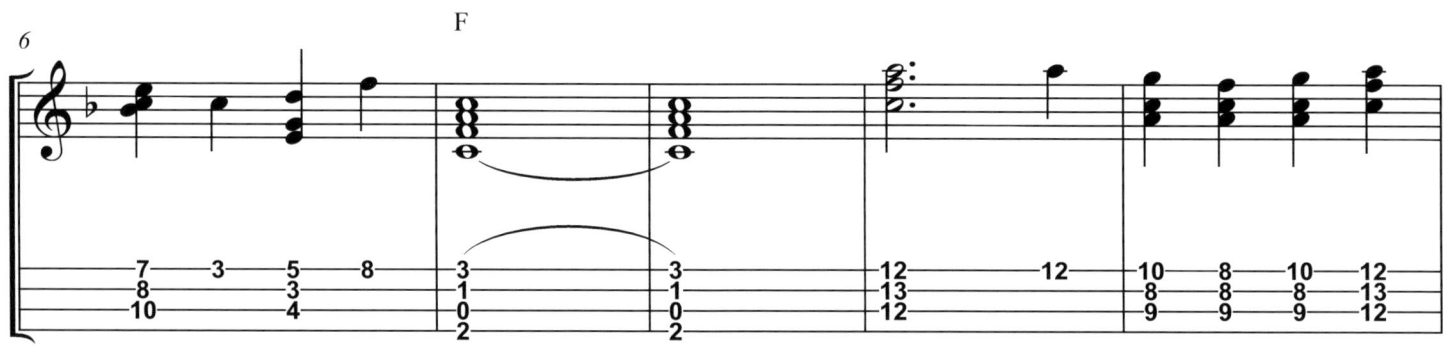

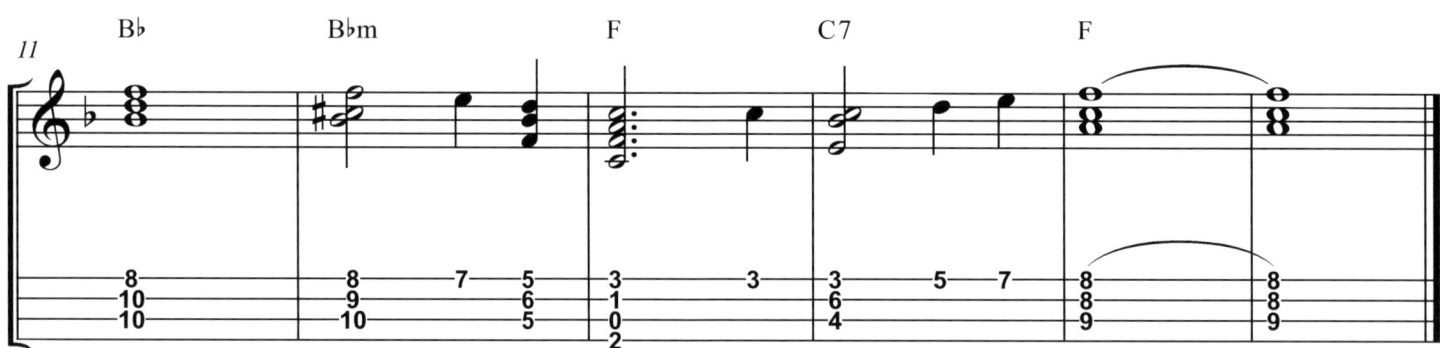

The Marine's Hymn

The author of this official American military song is unknown.

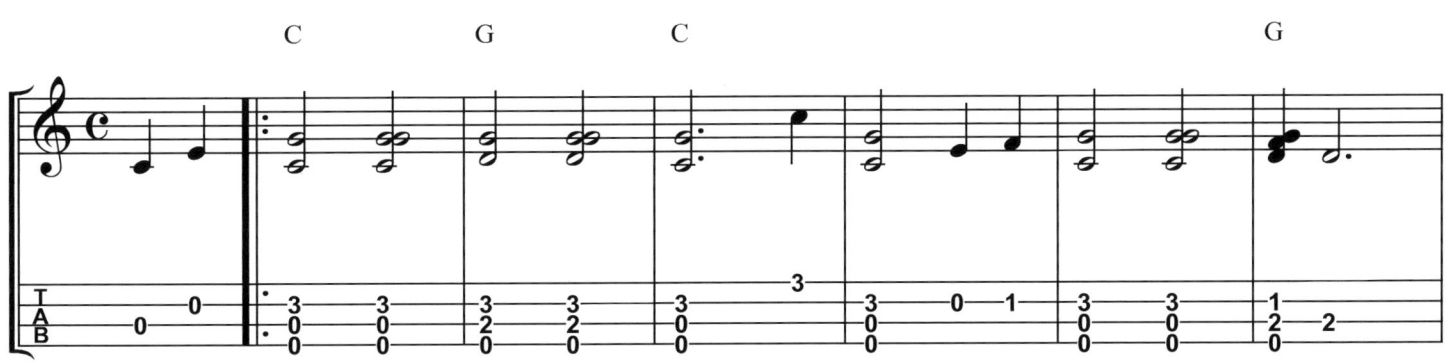
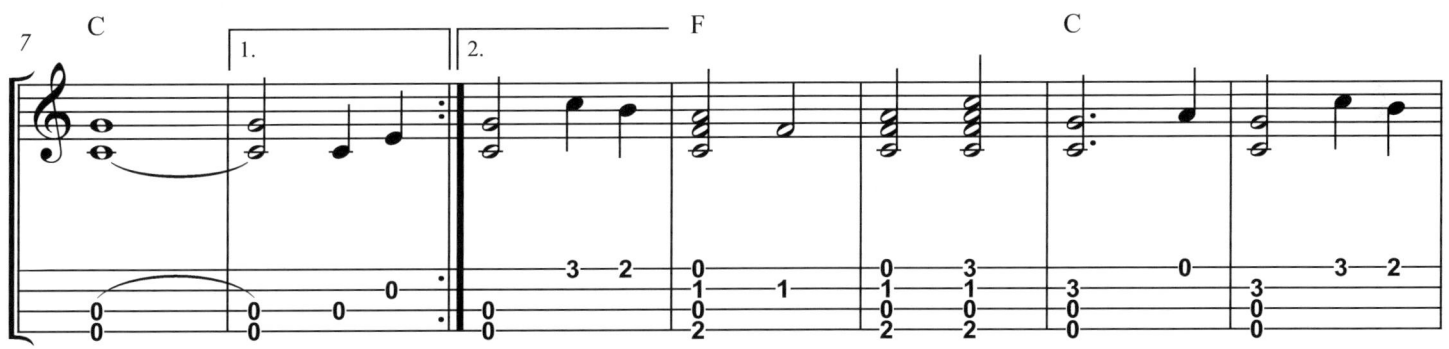
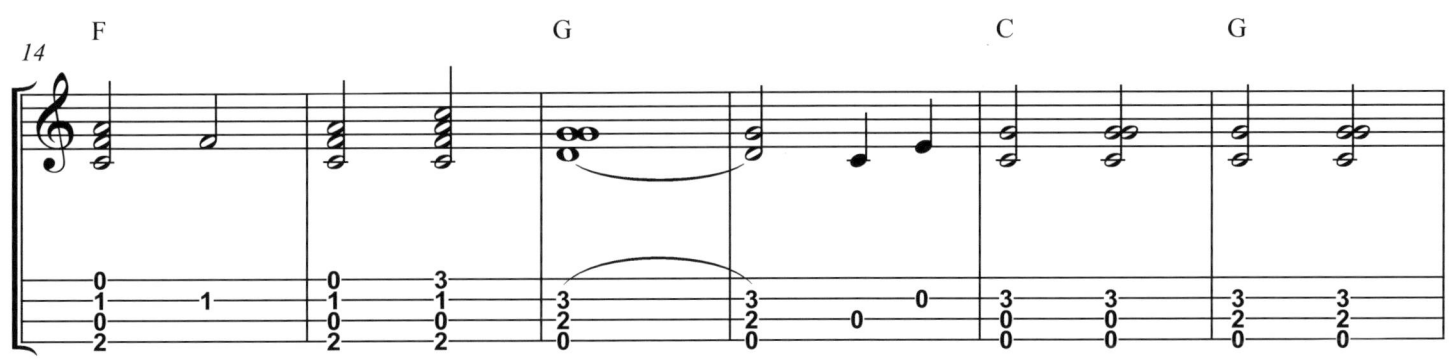
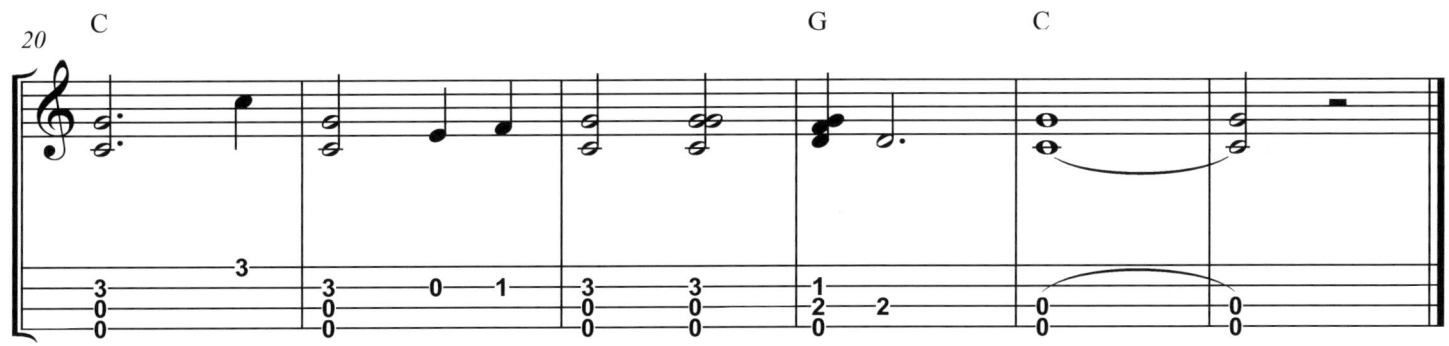

The Old Folks at Home

Here is another Stephen Foster song also known as "Swanee River," written in 1851. It was adopted as the state song of Florida in 1935.

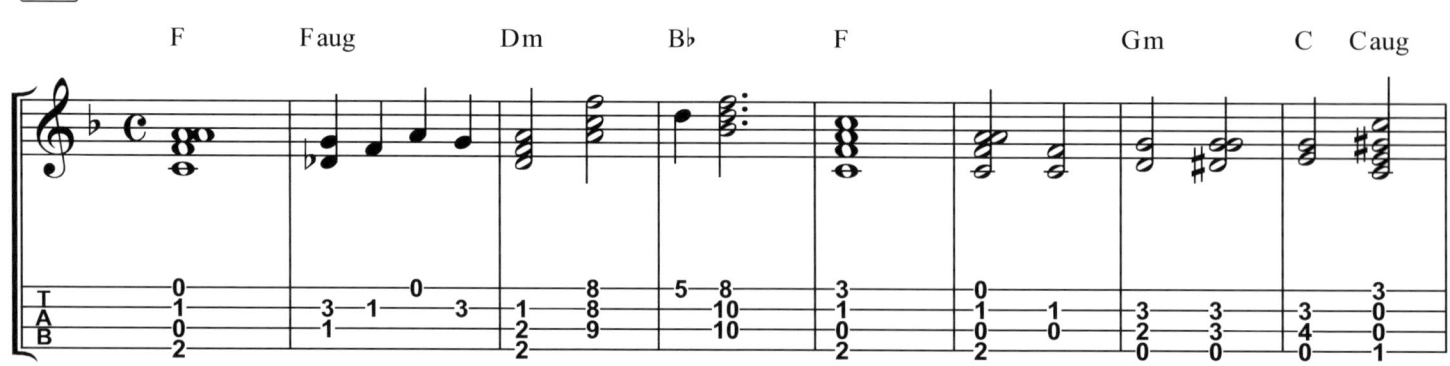

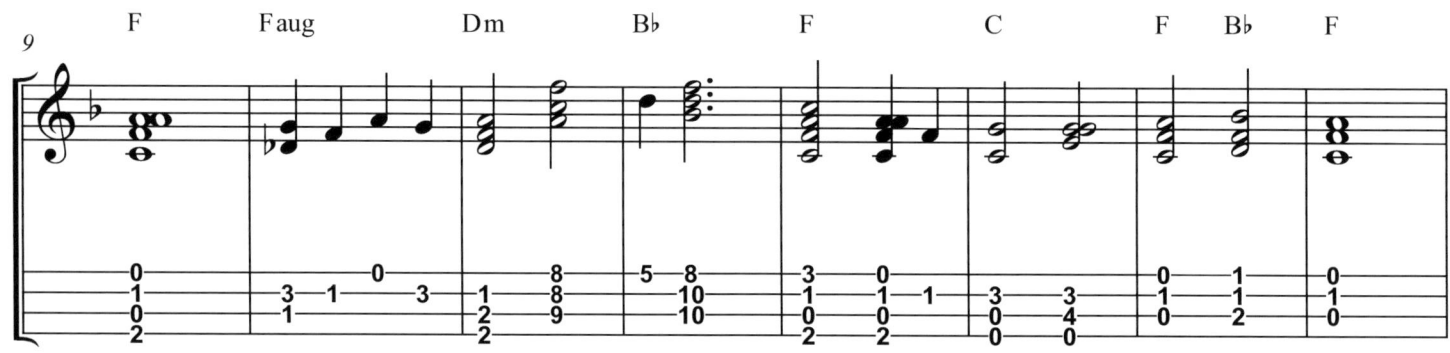

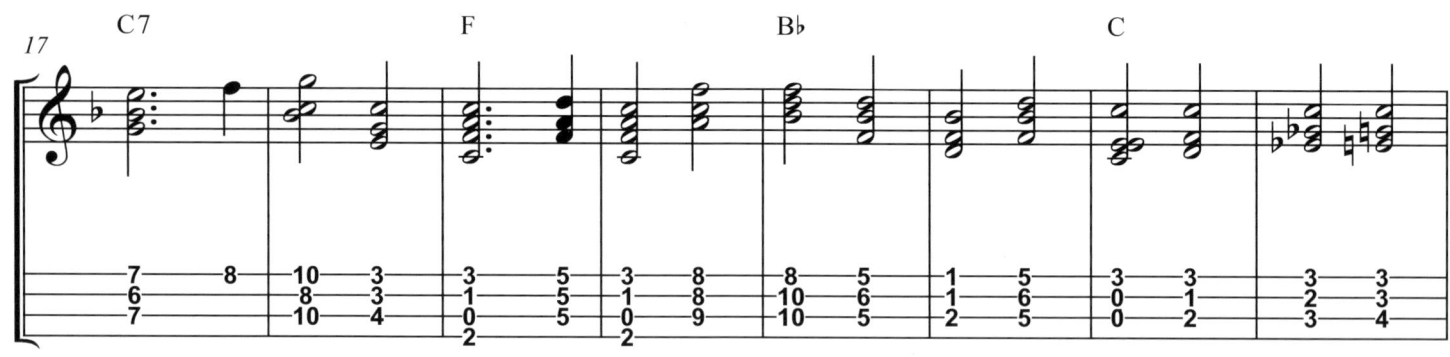

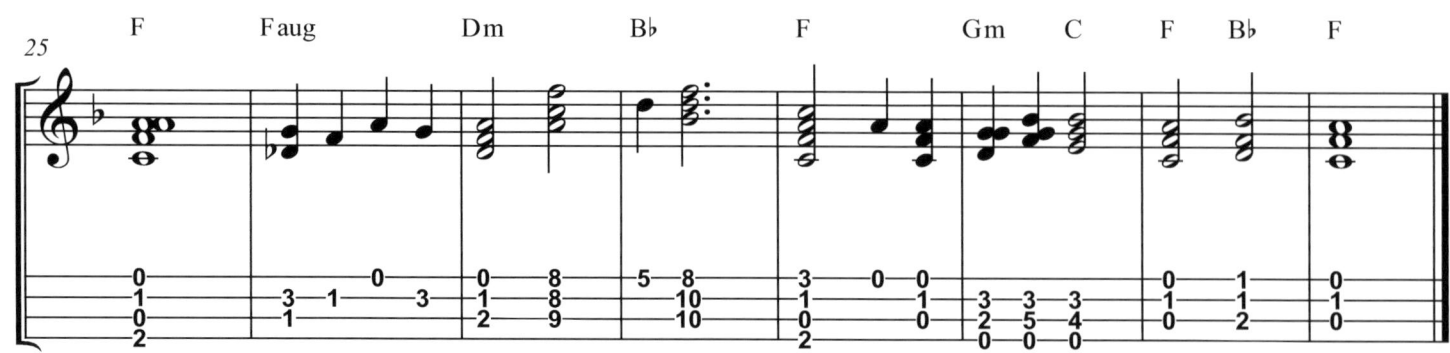

Peg of My Heart

Published in 1913 and popular thereafter.

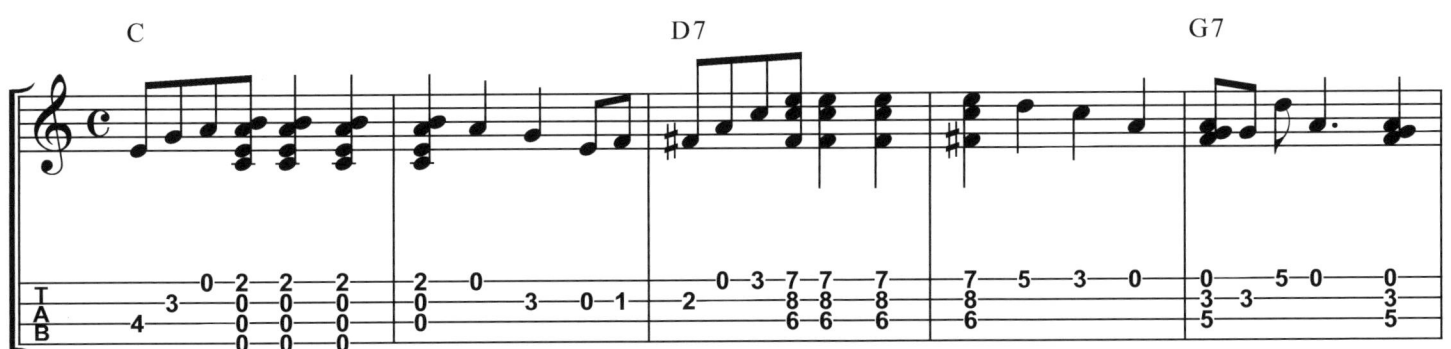

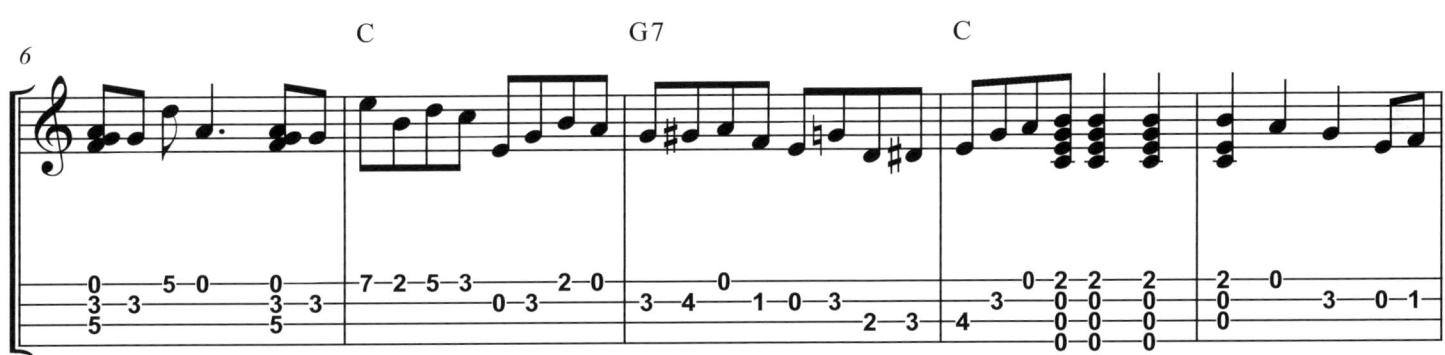

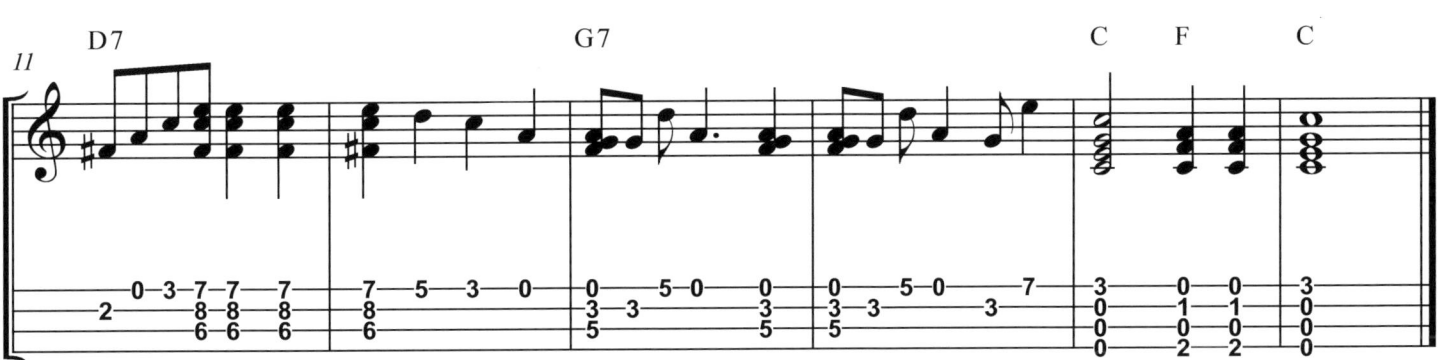

Scarborough Fair

This British ballad may date by as far back as the mid-1600s.

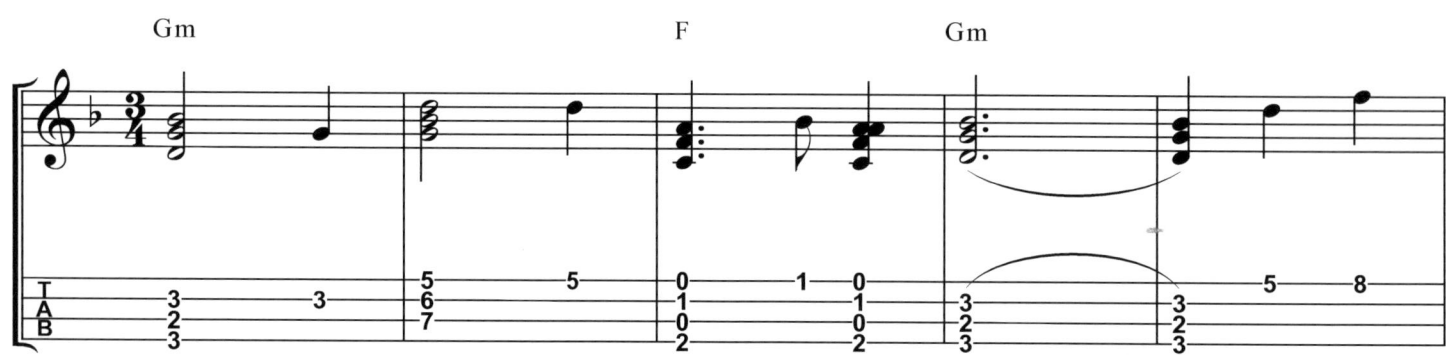

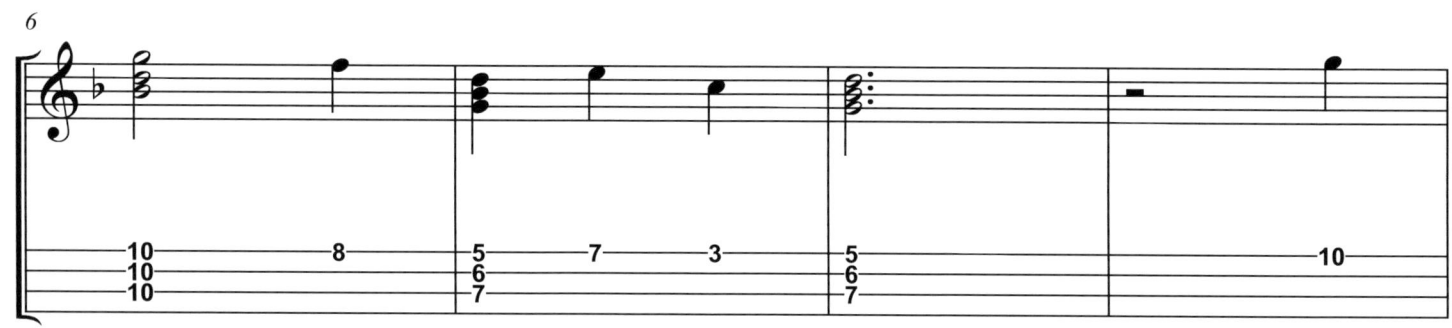

She'll Be Coming 'Round the Mountain

Based on an African-American spiritual, the lyrics were likely written in the late 1800s.

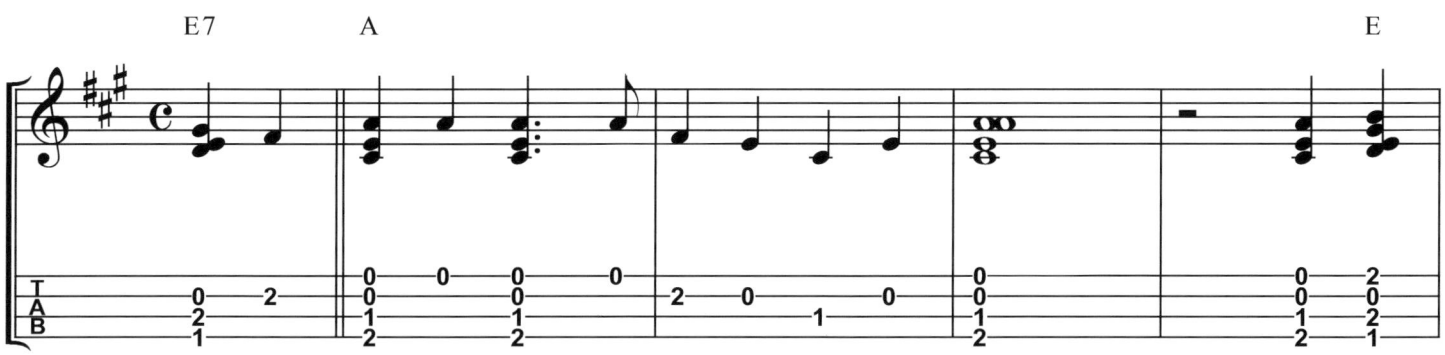
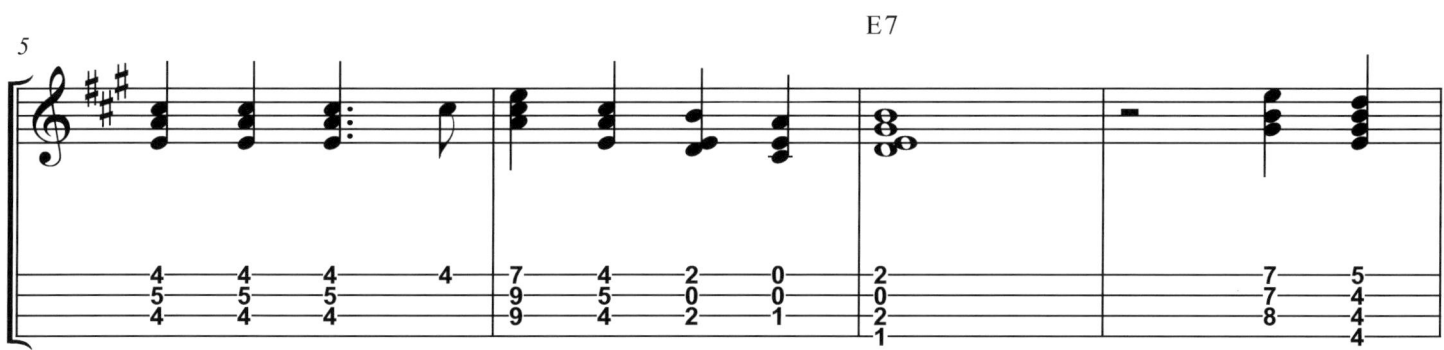
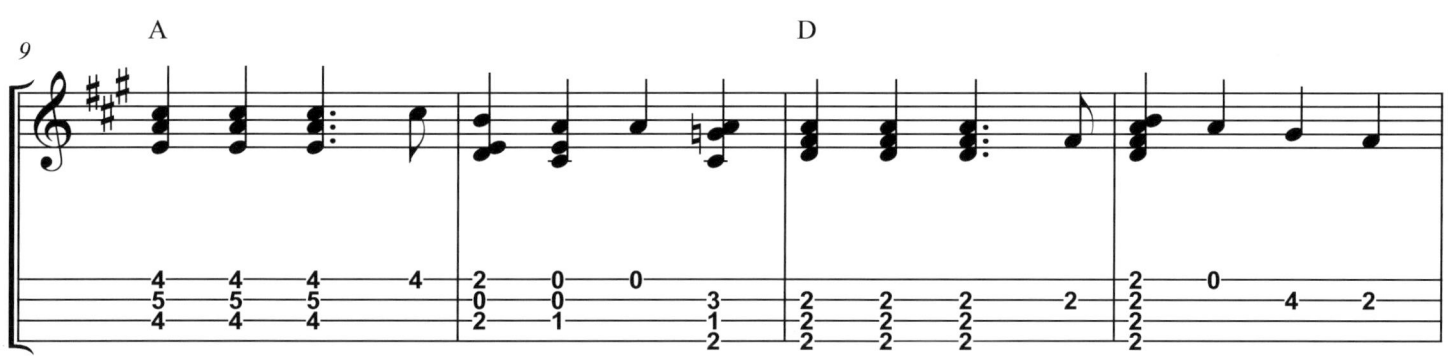
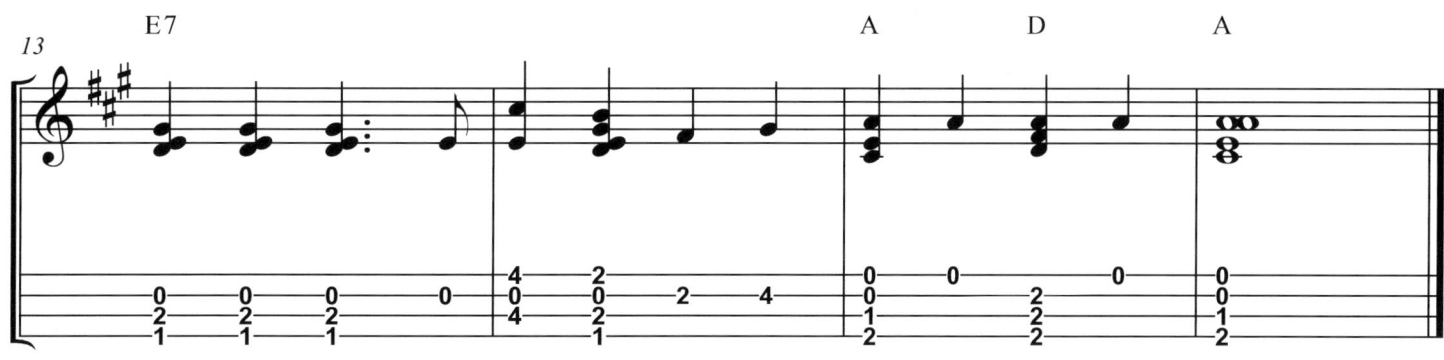

Shenendoah

This American folk song dates from the early 19th century.

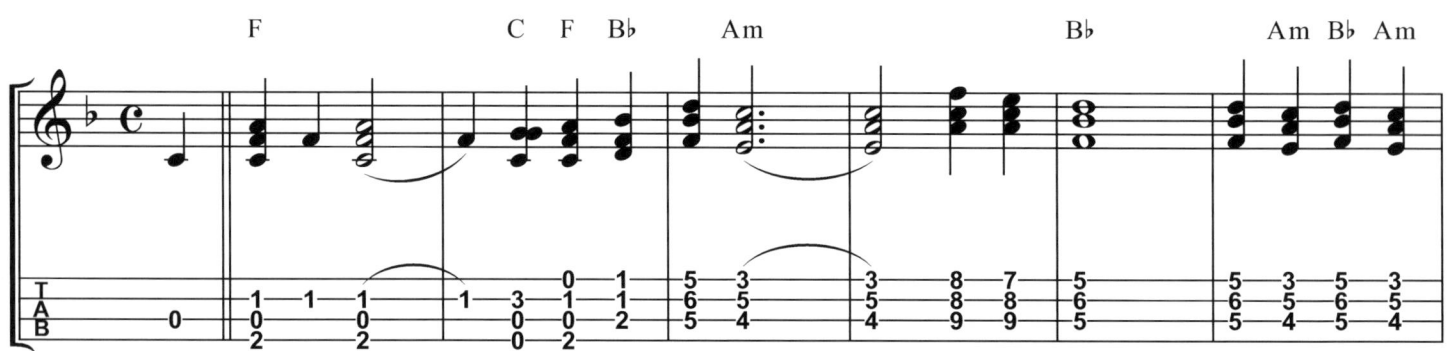

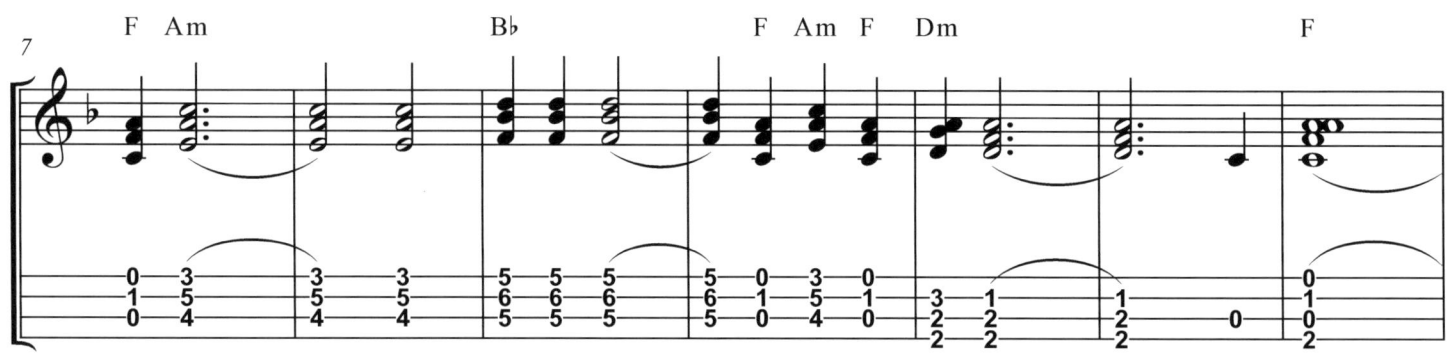

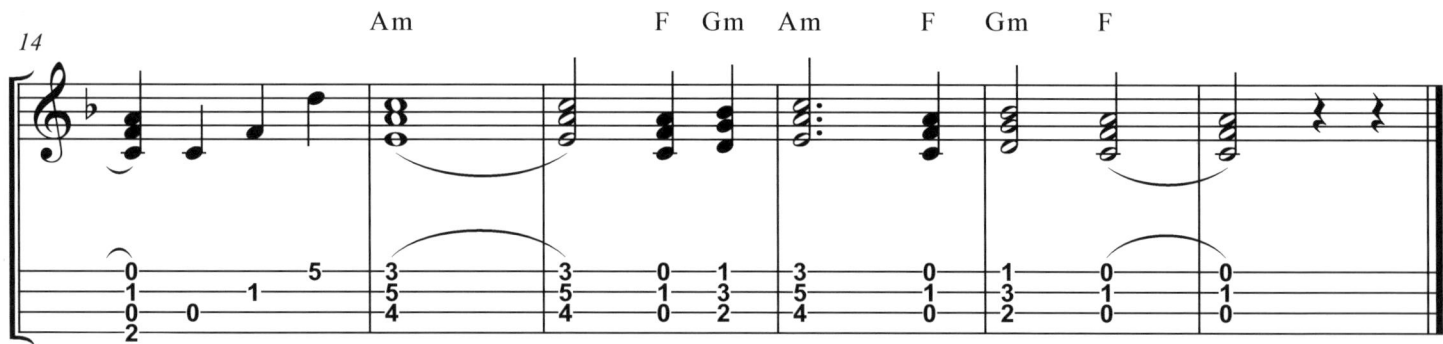

Auld Lang Syne

Scottish poet Robert Burns' 1788 poem has been become a required part of New Year's celebrations across the English speaking world.

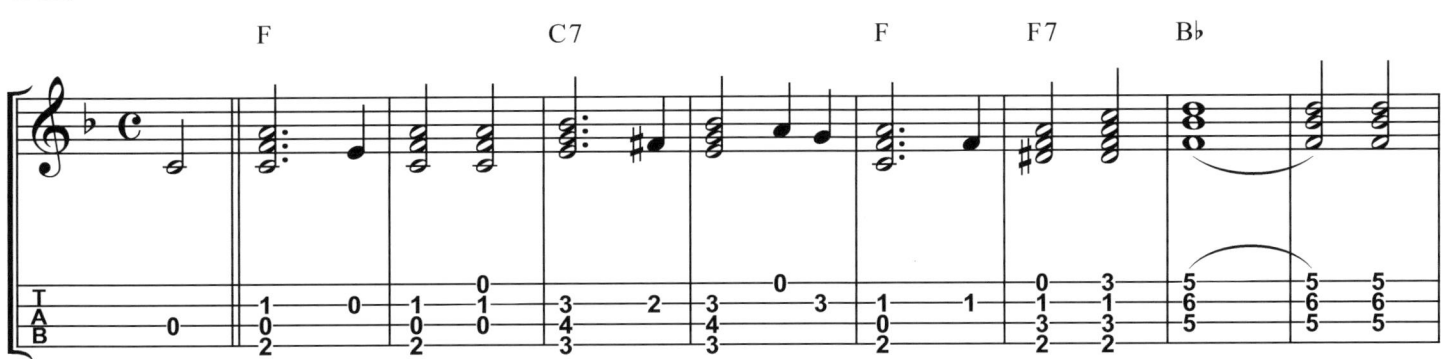

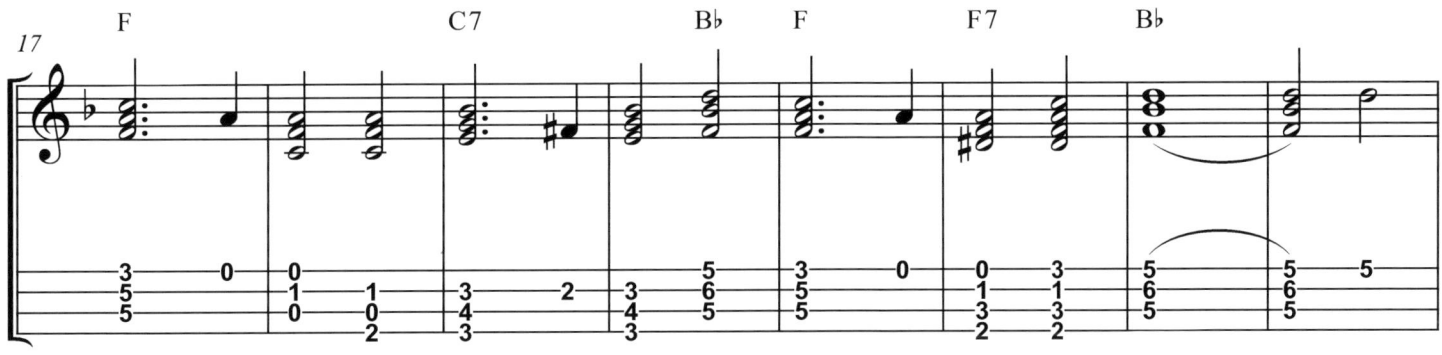

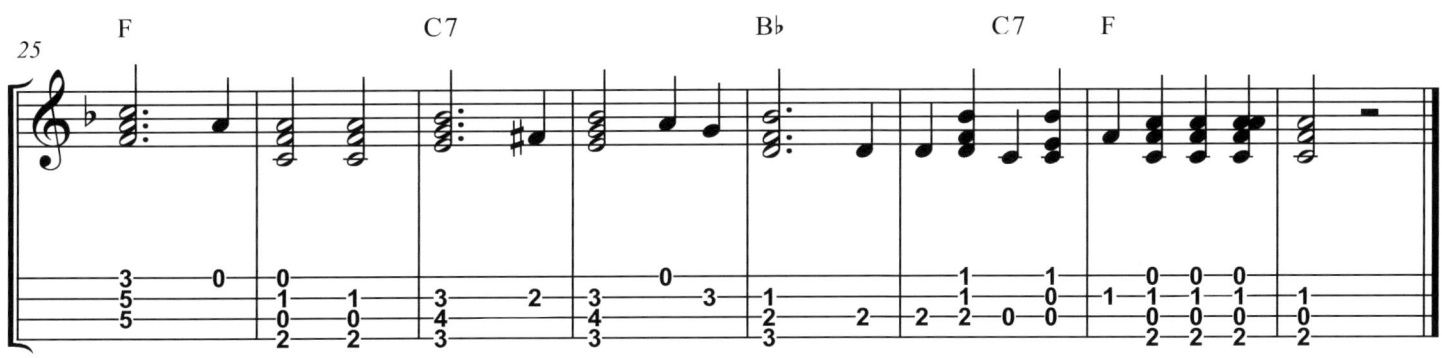

Conclusion

Congratulations! By completing this volume you are well on your way to making your ukulele playing a complete melody and rhythm style. Pick a good ukulele key and try arranging your favorite melodies. A simple Internet search will reveal the broad range of songs people are trying out on the uke. While most people use the ukulele only as an accompaniment to their singing, you are now prepared to try to play the melody and chords.

About the Author

Since 1985, Joe Carr has been a music instructor specializing in Bluegrass, Western Swing and Irish music in the Commercial Music program at South Plains College in Levelland, Texas. He was a director for Camp Bluegrass, a summer residential Music camp in its 26th year (2012).

In 1977, Joe joined the internationally known *Country Gazette* bluegrass band with banjo player Alan Munde and bluegrass legend Roland White. Joe appeared on three group albums, a solo album and numerous other recorded projects during his seven-year tenure with the band. In the 1990s, Carr and Munde formed a duo that toured extensively throughout the U.S., Canada and England and recorded two albums for Flying Fish/Rounder Records.

Joe has developed and appeared in over thirty instructional music videos for Mel Bay Publications and Texas Music & Video. He has written many instructional book/audio combinations for Mel Bay and has a growing number of videos available. Included are diverse titles such as *Western Swing Fiddle* MB20289M, *Mandolin Gospel* Tunes MB20554M and *School of Country Guitar* MB21645M.

Joe was a regular columnist for Flatpicking Guitar Magazine and Mandolin Magazine.

In 1996, the Texas Tech University Press published *Prairie Nights to Neon Lights: The Story of Country Music in West Texas* by Carr and Munde. Joe can be seen and heard at acousticmusician.com/JoeCarr.html Joe plays Mendel ukuleles.

In 2008, Joe received the International Bluegrass Music Association's (IBMA) Distinguished Achievement Award for his career-long efforts in support of bluegrass music.